# How to Write
# A Family History

*The Lives and Times of Our Ancestors*

# How to Write

# A Family History

## the Lives and Times of Our Ancestors

## Terrick V H FitzHugh

Alphabooks · A & C Black  London

First published 1988 by
Alphabooks Ltd, Sherborne, Dorset
A subsidiary of
A & C Black (Publishers) Ltd
35 Bedford Row, London WC1

ISBN 0 7136 3078 7


British Library Cataloguing in Publication Data

FitzHugh, Terrick V.H.
    How to write a family history.
    1. Great Britain. Genealogies. Compilation
    & publishing — Amateurs' manuals.
    I. Title
    808'.066929021

    ISBN 0-7136-3078-7

*The picture on the title page is an illustration by*
*Phiz — 'Christmas dance at a country house', 1856.*

Photosetting by L.P. & T.S. Ltd, Langport, Somerset
Printed by Butler & Tanner Ltd, Frome, Somerset

# Contents

To
my Wife,
Mary,
whose interests lie fortunately
in the present

*The retrieving of these forgotten Things from Oblivion in some sort resembles the Art of a Conjuror who makes those walke and appeare that have layen in their graves many hundreds of yeares; and to represent as it were to the eie the places, Customes and Fashions that were of old Times.*

*John Aubrey*

# 1

# From family tree to family history

Getting on for sixty years ago, my father proudly showed me the family tree that he and his brother-in-law had spent years in researching. They had just heard that the College of Arms had checked and approved it. As I perused the tall trunk of our twelve generations I noticed many Christian names familiar to me through being handed down the centuries to some of my living relatives, one of them indeed to myself. I read the dates under the names and saw that, though some members of the family had died in childhood, many had been septuagenarians and octogenarians; and this set me wondering about the lives they had lived and the kind of people they had been. But seemingly all that was known of each of them now was their dates of baptism, marriage and burial, and a few place-names.

Being young and impressionable I felt how sad that was, and how very badly it reflected on us for neglecting to keep their memory alive. Those people, our own forebears, had lived and loved, experienced the stresses of earning their livelihood, bringing up their children, and coping with the pressures of their day. They had passed down to us our family name, our position in life, our life-blood itself; and we had forgotten all about them! I felt ashamed. Also the dark thought oppressed me that similar oblivion was clearly to be my own lot.

That it was too late to do anything about it, that all knowledge of our forebears was lost for ever, I took for granted. From my father's and uncle's success with the family tree I could understand that the Church of England had kept records of their christenings, weddings and funerals, but it never for one moment occurred to me that, though we ourselves had kept no memorials of them, some evidence of the people they had been and the lives they had lived might yet exist somewhere or other and be discoverable.

Then, four years later, chance suddenly gave me a few brief glimpses into my family's past. I was browsing in the library of what was then the British Drama League. My eye fell on six volumes of the memoirs of the early nineteenth-century actress, Fanny Kemble, three of them entitled *Record of a Girlhood*, and three *Records of Later Life*. According to reminiscent chat in my family, my great-great-aunt Emily had been a friend of Fanny Kemble's. 'I wonder,' I thought sceptically, 'if she was really enough of a friend to be mentioned in her memoirs.' I pulled out the last of each three-volume set and turned to their indexes. Sure enough, there she was, on a number of pages ('her face expressive of both intelligence and sensibility'). Not only that; her mother, my great-great-grandmother, also appeared frequently ('the funniest and the kindest old maniac I am acquainted with'). I borrowed the volumes and copied out all the family mentions into a new manuscript book, which I resolved to devote to any future FitzHugh memorabilia I might chance upon. I was not really hopeful, and certainly had no idea that I had taken the first step on what was to be a life-long quest.

Because of my lack of belief in the possibility of discovering much about my family's past lives, I dissipated my energy for several years in the genealogical pursuit of tracing my ancestors through every line of ascent, male and female. In a few generations these forerunners became, as they always do, so numerous that it was impossible to look for anything more about them than just their names and three vital dates, which made the operation as superficial as collecting train numbers; so when discoveries about my FitzHugh family's lives began to accumulate, I abandoned Total Descent research as mere Ancestor Spotting.

In those early days of my genealogical and family history interests, I seldom encountered more than three or four fellow searchers up on the narrow balconies and down in the basement at Somerset House. In my lonely delvings I would have thought anyone joking who prophesied that one day thousands of ancestor searchers would descend like locusts upon the General Register indexes and Census Returns, oblige the authorities to open larger premises, and still complain of overcrowding. At that period, the idea that my seemingly eccentric hobby entitled me to any special facilities never occurred to me.

Though it was from a printed book that I received my first encouragement to search my family's past, since then printed sources have supplied no more than a minute part of the 'foreground' evidence I have discovered, by which I mean actual mentions of their names. Virtually all my finds have been made from old manuscripts in public record repositories and have been of the family moving, not in the company of celebrities like Fanny Kemble, but among people as little known to fame as themselves.

In 1943 I became a member of the Society of Genealogists, which was housed at that time on an upper floor in Malet Street, and had only half as many members as several county family history societies can boast today; and it would be years yet before L.G. Pine would write the first of the present flood of genealogical guidebooks.

One piece of luck I did have. Bedfordshire, where my earliest-known ancestors lived, was one of only half-a-dozen counties that had a County Record Office. Towards the end of the war I managed to get a posting to the RAF station at Henlow, where I could catch a bus into Bedford. In the tiny search room I was helped by Miss Joyce Godber, the archivist, who later wrote a history of the county. In fact, she offered to recommend me for the job of her assistant as soon as I was demobbed, but her mention of the salary brought that project to an end. There and at the Public Record Office in Chancery Lane I continued on my solitary way, turning up one piece of the FitzHugh past after another, fitting them together and getting a steadily clearer view of my family's fortunes as they threaded their way through the centuries. My discoveries were a constant source of surprise and delight to me. Even today when I am well aware of the riches of English historical archives, I am amazed and amused at the intimate and personal nature of some of the revelations of my family that have been preserved for hundreds of years, some of them quite unmentionable here by anyone as old-fashioned as I am.

Concurrently with my researches I pursued my reading of history, filling in the backgrounds to my ancestors' activities and noting them down as carefully as I did actual mentions of the family, because I knew that it would be decades before I could start to work the information into a narrative history. Today, ranged along my bookshelves, stand twenty 500-sheet volumes of transcribed evidence, the product of my researches. As I survey those tomes with some complacence, my dearest impossible wish is that my late father could return to see the stirrings of life that I have breathed into his skeletal pedigree. But who knows? Now perhaps he and my other ancestors go strolling together in the Elysian Fields, swapping reminiscences of their experiences here below.

Successful beyond my wildest dreams in uncovering my family's past, and having now spent six years in writing up my discoveries as narrative history, I feel the urge to share what the whole enjoyable experience has taught me. But I am giving way to the impulse only because of three considerations. The first is that, of all the aspects of family history discussed in publications, work on the final narrative product has so far hardly been touched on, certainly no treatment in detail. The second is that so many so-called family histories show no attempt by their authors to place their ancestors in their contemporary contexts, and so are not histories at all but little more than bare family trees rewritten as narrative. Of course, some researchers, despite their best endeavours, may have been unable to find anything worth adding to their genealogical data, and it would be unreasonable to carp at their setting them out in readable form; but, judging by the property-owning or professional status evident in many such 'histories', it is plain that lack of discoverable evidence is not the reason for their tunnel-vision treatment. The real reason, I am convinced, is that many genealogists are under the same illusion as I once was; they have no idea of the wealth of biographical material waiting to be discovered. The third consideration that made me think it worthwhile to describe my research and writing experiences is that I started with no family papers and only a handful turned up later, so that virtually all my discoveries have been made where anyone can go searching, in record repositories and libraries open to the general public, which I have no reason to think house any more evidence of my family than of any other family of roughly the same kind.

My 'kind of family' — that limitation does have a certain relevance. In recent years I have lectured a number of times on the subject 'From Family Tree to Family History', and on two occasions I have had a student come up to me afterwards and say that he or she expected that as so much evidence has survived about my family, they must have been 'more important' than theirs; so that, in spite of all my encouragement, they were not optimistic of finding much about their own folk. They were of course alluding to what Lord David Cecil called 'that distressing subject', social class. So it may be reassuring to give an outline of the varying walks of life that were trodden through the centuries by the family about which I have found so much.

Until the sixteenth century my forebears were what historians term 'lesser gentry', lords of small manors in Bedfordshire and Buckinghamshire; but then my particular branch of the family, descended from a younger son of a younger son and therefore receiving only the left-overs of inheritance, made their living for two generations as maltsters in the same counties. Early in the seventeenth century, a fourteen-year-old ancestor was apprenticed in London and became a hosier on Old London Bridge, in which occupation he was followed by his son and one of his grandsons. At the beginning of the eighteenth century, my next ancestor entered the maritime service of the East India Company. He was succeeded by a son trading in Turkey and next by an East India Company supercargo at Canton, both of whom retired to Hampshire in early middle age, the latter becoming a Member of Parliament. His successor, a country clergyman in Sussex, was followed by a barrister in the civil service, and then by my father, another country parson. The scope, however, of the history I am writing embraces also my ancestors' siblings, thereby including also a sixteenth-century lawyer, an early eighteenth-century linendraper, mid eighteenth-century traders in Syria, China and the West Indies, a midshipman in the Napoleonic Wars, and a solicitor and two army officers in Victorian times.

10

In my narrative history of this not very 'important' family I have so far reached from the Middle Ages down to the year 1768, filling the typescript equivalent of about 350 printed book pages. Their written story so far tells of fairly ordinary people making their way, generation by generation, through various economic, religious, political and social phases of English history, namely the Reformation, Puritan Revolution, Civil War, rise of party politics, expansion of overseas trade, and the territorial accumulation of the early British Empire. It will go on — once this present book is finished — to reflect the Napoleonic Wars, the introduction of steam power, liberation of the slaves, church controversies, the Crimean War, and the defence of the Empire. After that, I plan to come to a stop with the grand climax of my own birth, because I find the prospect of writing autobiography altogether too daunting, and anyway feel that a subjective final section would make an incongruous conclusion to a conscientiously objective history.

For tracing a family's genealogical descent, the sources of evidence are nearly all to be found within a certain limited range of records. Manuals of genealogy can list the titles of these sources and describe their contents; but what is possible and sufficient for a process of which the end product is just a chart, is impossible for a family history describing the experiences of generations of people who lived infinitely various lives in almost as infinitely various surroundings and conditions. No source list could contain them. Also, mere descriptions of the documents in each class of record would fall short of what is needed. The only medium through which we can gain experience of the colours, flavours and infinitely intricate patterns of peoples' lives in social conditions utterly different from ours and vanished forever, is the actual wording of the documents that recorded them at the time. In addition to the bare facts, for which the researcher has sought them, they convey the attitude behind their being written, the atmosphere of their period and unforeseeable concomitant details, all of which make up the very stuff of history. The only way to convey them when discussing the writing of family history is by quotation. Therefore, in the chapters that follow, quotation will be the medium of the message.

To illustrate each class of record, a choice titbit could be picked out of its entire range over the whole country. W.E. Tate did that most effectively in *The Parish Chest*, and D.J Steel in Vol.I of the *National Index of Parish Registers*, but any reader of those works who might be wondering what his chance would be of finding a single item of such high interest for his own family must feel it somewhat similar to that of his Premium Bond coming up. My purpose in selection here is different from Tate's and Steel's. It aims to show not only the quality of some of the existing documentary evidence, but also the quantity of such evidence that a historian can expect to find for his own individual family. To do this, my choice of quotations will be on the lines of a case study, drawn entirely from those discovered for one single branch of one family, my own.

Because of the infinite variety of family trails through history, there is no such thing as a typical family, but because of my family's middling status they are, for the purposes of example, less atypical than many others that could be chosen; they cut a central swathe through society, and of course they have the essential merit for this purpose of having been thoroughly researched. A quick flick through these pages of this book will show a quotation at most of the openings, so when I say that all of them together comprise only a tiny percentage of the total documentary evidence I have discovered, they will, I hope, convey some idea of the treasure awaiting discovery by the biographical researcher of any line of descent. Some of the documents from which I quote will be directly applicable to many readers' cases, and most of the others will, I hope, suggest ideas for searches in parallel sources.

To sum up, in writing this book I have tried:

1   To persuade the reader of the possibility of researching and writing a truly narrative family history as distinct from a mere narrative family tree or album of family miscellanea;
2   To convey an idea of the biographical and background sources available to a family history researcher;
3   To show by quotation the rich period colour and flavour of the documentary evidence and its narrative possibilities;
4   To show by example the surprising wealth of biographical information it is possible to discover for one single branch of one family;
5   To discuss practical writing problems inherent in the very specialised art of family historiography.

# 2

# Terms used in this book

In ancestry research, amateurs greatly outnumber professionals, so it is not surprising that its technical terms are often used in a loose colloquial sense instead of with genealogical exactitude. The following glossary should help to avoid misunderstandings in reading this book.

*Ancestor, Ancestress* One's ancestor or ancestress is a person from whom one is actually descended, not just any bygone member of the family. It is incorrect to write (as I have recently seen done) of someone as a descendant of John Keats, the poet. As he had no offspring, he is nobody's ancestor and therefore has no descendants. The remark was made about a descendant of his brother, who was the real ancestor.

*Ancestry* This term, unlike *Family* includes forebears in all lines of descent, male and female, which are usually set out on a Total Blood Descent chart. One often hears people say they can trace their family back to the Conquest. What they should be saying is that they can trace their *ancestry* back that far, because they are doing it, not exclusively through their male-line descent (their family), but through female lines. Only a very small number of present-day families can trace their male line back to the Conquest.

There are unfortunately no terms in English to mean 'a bygone male or female member of a family other than an ancestor or ancestress'. If there were, I should be frequently using them in this book. As things are, however, I just speak about ancestors and ancestresses, and leave it to the common sense of the reader to understand that in most cases what I am saying about them applies equally well to their siblings. For instance, when I say, 'Ancestors' religious opinions may be revealed in their Last Wills and Testaments', that is obviously equally true of the opinions of other members of the family.

*Armiger* A person entitled to bear heraldic arms.

*Family* In social conversation, we speak and think of our maternal uncles and aunts as members of our family, but in genealogical terminology they are not. In genealogy, a family consists of people of the same surname and blood, i.e. those descended in an all-male line from a common male ancestor. A family may consist of a number of collateral branches stretching down from brothers. This is known as an Extended Family. It is quite incorrect to speak of a person's maternal lines of ancestry as branches of his family. They are different families.

*Family history* Basically, a family history consists of overlapping biographies of members of a family in its progress through the centuries. The overlapping is horizontal between siblings and vertical between parents and issue. Family history tells of their activities and the outside events and influences that impinged upon their lives; it places them in their various contexts, domestic, occupational, local, social and national-historical; it seeks to explain the reasons for any changes in family circumstances and to describe their consequences.

*Family tree* A chart showing one or more male-line descents from a single male ancestor. It should not be confused with a Total Blood Descent Chart, which shows a person's ancestry through all male and female lines of descent.

*Genealogy* and *Genealogist* At one time, the words 'genealogy' and 'family history' were used interchangeably to cover the whole study of ancestry, but the need has been realised to distinguish between two separate activities. The term 'genealogy' is now confined to the tracing of descents for the compilation of Family Tree and Total Blood Descent charts; and 'family history' applies to the researching and writing of family histories. In this book, when genealogy and family history need to be spoken of together, the inclusive term 'Ancestry Research' will be used.

*Historiography* Though sometimes used to mean the history of history writing, the term is here used in its *Oxford English Dictionary* (OED) sense of the writing of history. Family historiography, the subject of this book, consists of the processes, covering several generations of a family, of biographical research, note-taking, interpretation and narrative composition.

*Primary Evidence* This is provided by documents or other artifacts created at or near the time of the events they record, and solely for the purpose for which the class of record itself was created. It had then nothing to do with genealogy, family history or any other extraneous use. Though primary evidence is more valuable than secondary (see below), it is often less than self-explanatory, so that its interpretation calls for some knowledge of the class of record itself and its background.

*Quotations* For reasons I shall go into in detail in the chapter on Writing the Narrative, the quotations given in this book from historical sources have been modernised in spelling, capitalisation, punctuation and paragraphing.

*Secondary Evidence* This is provided by writings falling outside the definition of Primary Evidence, and usually created at a period removed clearly from the events they record. Examples are histories and family trees (see *Primary Evidence*). There are, however, grey areas between primary and secondary evidence, where the writings are contemporaneous, such as newspaper reports, autobiographies and histories of the authors' own times, but have been subjected to personal evaluation or written with extraneous purposes in mind.

*Sibling* A word surprisingly not to be found in many small dictionaries. When the OED was first compiled it applied to any family relative, but now means a brother or sister.

*Transcript* A copy, made in the copyist's own handwriting or typing, of the wording and spelling of a document. Unlike a photocopy, it does not reproduce the original style of handwriting. It may be abbreviated by omissions, which must be indicated by dots or other signs.

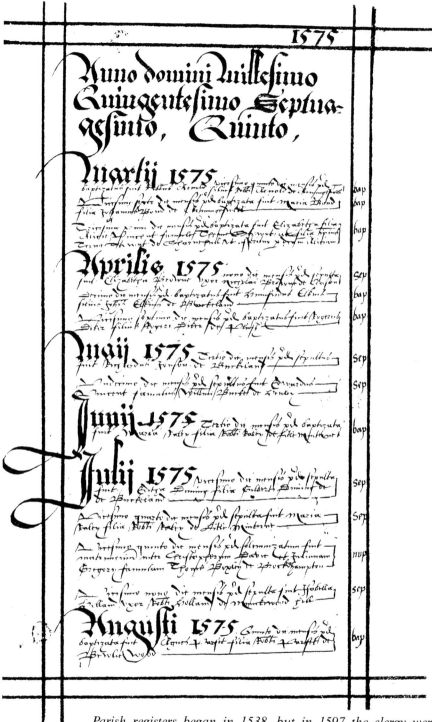

*Parish registers began in 1538, but in 1597 the clergy were ordered to copy all their previous entries, which had been on loose sheets of paper, into bound volumes. So this page is from the first register book of Buckland Newton, Dorset. Baptisms, marriages and burials appear on the same pages.*

# 3

# Research

A family history cannot be written solely from the results of genealogical research. Exploration of a far wider and deeper type is required; so something must be said on this subject before we can come to any discussion of writing. However, even research is not the first step. A certain amount of preliminary planning is needed, which we will now consider.

The first decision to be taken is on the question: who are going to be included within the history's scope and who left out? Personally, I decided to include in my narrative every member of each generation of my own branch of the family, i.e. my male-line ancestors and ancestresses and the ancestors' siblings. As a line has to be drawn somewhere, I drew mine to exclude the careers of sisters' husbands. They were, after all, members of other families and therefore the responsibility of other historians. In my history I mention them only when their activities can be seen to affect their wives or other members of my family.

You may think you would prefer to confine yourself to just your actual ancestor and ancestress in each generation, but such a course would be a self-inflicted deprivation. Remember that to relate their stories you have to place them within their contexts; and their closest human context for much of their lives was their nearest and dearest at home. As most genealogists will be aware from noting the names of witnesses on marriage certificates and of executors and beneficiaries in wills, brotherly and sisterly links often persisted throughout life. Sometimes siblings worked together; sometimes they quarrelled and went to law; sometimes the financial situation of one was transformed by the will or intestacy of another; and some of these situations may only be discoverable by researching the siblings separately. So writing the life of one member of the family in isolation can only result in an incomplete picture; and it will certainly not produce a *family* history. And there is another, very practical reason for including siblings. Your researches into one ancestor may fail to turn up anything really interesting, and then you will be thankful to have his siblings to fill what would otherwise have been a yawning gap.

The principle of including no one more distantly related than siblings does in practice allow the partial inclusion of ancestors' nephews and nieces, because of course their births were important events in the lives of their parents (the siblings); and some things that these children did later, but within their parents' lifetime, such as dying in childhood or getting themselves into trouble, will also have affected their parents. In one chapter of my history, which I shall be reproducing here as an example of the practice of my principles, the worries that an ancestor's brother and sister are caused by their respective offspring play a major part.

Some people have asked me, slightly aggressively, why I am writing the history of an all-male line of descent. Why not an all-female line? Could I not then be quite sure that I was dealing with a true biological descent? The questioner insinuates that some of my FitzHugh ancestresses may have passed off on their unobservant husbands children actually conceived in secret adultery. In the complete absence of any evidence or even suspicion to such effect, any attention I paid to such a smear would be an insult to good women long in their graves. However, I was well aware that the implied aspersion on my ancestresses was not the real reason for questioning my male-line family history. Behind it was a feeling that the female line of descent was being excluded just because it was female, and that calls for a serious answer.

For the historian, it is not just that, in the context of our social past, male-line family history has advantages but that all-female lines have great disadvantages. The least of the male-line advantages is the convenience for readers in the continuity of family name and background, constant changes in these basic data being liable to become confusing. Although a family has always been liable to be found moving from one town or village to another, there would be a family-history reason for the move, which would be interesting in itself, and such moves would be unlikely to happen as frequently as would be the trend if the author kept diverting the reader to a son-in-law's family. A far greater thematic advantage is the social continuity conferred by the historical role of the husband/father as breadwinner. His occupation decided the family's social status; his sons tended to be put to careers of the same standing; and the walk of life into which each generation was born was its most pervasive nurtural influence. But what fundamentally makes the male-line story the only practical one is the sad fact that, owing to the social and legal position of women in past ages, and in spite of recent work done by 'herstorians', almost all the surviving documentary evidence is of the activities of men. So family history inevitably becomes a tale about fathers, sons and brothers, with mothers, daughters and sisters in supporting roles, and widows occasionally taking centre stage. That being the case, to make a daughter in each generation the reason for cutting short the story of the men of one family in order to move away to the men of another would be difficult to bring off artistically — and narrative history is an art.

The following diagram illustrates what I have found in practice to be a workable set of characters for a family history. Laying down in advance a general principle of the work's boundaries concentrates the mind during research and, at the writing stage, keeps the story moving forward along its central line. It does not mean that the historian should never allow himself to be drawn aside to mention a particularly interesting second cousin. Guide lines must not become tram lines.

**Suggested scope of a family history**

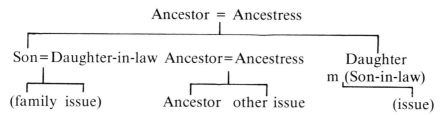

The careers of persons shown in brackets are recommended to be included only in so far as they affect the unbracketed members of the family.

When embarking upon research to fill the initially desert stretches between the genealogical milestones of baptism, marriage and burial you may ask yourself the question: 'What exactly is it I am looking for?', and be embarrassingly stumped for an answer. In genealogy you know what you need to find, namely those milestones; but in the rest of a person's lifespan any events at all may have happened, and you have no idea what they are likely to have been. There is, however, a systematic method of going about the search which is likely to uncover nearly all evidence still extant. It can be summarised as follows:

1. A more detailed re-examination of genealogical sources already researched.
2. Widening research to include those records that genealogists are aware of but usually consult only if their standard ones fail to reveal what they need for the purposes of their descent.
3. Reading published material for historical backgrounds and contexts.

1749

A Rate made for ÿ Repairing of ÿ Church of Hazelbery
Bryant for ÿ year ————————— 1749

| | £ | s | d | | £ | s | d |
|---|---|---|---|---|---|---|---|
| Jos whitt | 5 | 0 | | Dock: mitchel | 3 | 10 | |
| Mr Bingham | 0 | 2 | 2 | Mrs Light | 2 | 6 | |
| Mr Brient | 1 | 2 | | Mr Loder | 2 | 7 | 2 |
| Mr welson | 2 | 1 | | Mr Robert Bridge | 2 | 5 | 3/4 |
| Mount plesent | 1 | 2 | | Mr Robert Hill | 1 | 5 | 3 |
| Stockfield | 1 | 8 | | Joseph Rooles | 0 | 2 | |
| Jockets farem | 5 | 6 | | Mr Richard Hill | 4 | 3 | |
| Wedow Pope | 0 | 3 | 2 | Joseph Hawkens | 1 | 0 | |
| mrs fill | 0 | 10 | 2 | Edward Hennell | 0 | 9 | 3/1 |
| Mr Bolls | 1 | 5 | | Cundit Carlor | 0 | 10 | 2 |
| Joseph muston | 0 | 9 | | Mr Richard Chapman | 0 | 4 | |
| Robert Boyd | 1 | 4 | | Thomas fill | 0 | 1 | 2 |
| Mr Caselman | 1 | 1 | | 4th Snooks | 1 | 2 | |
| Christopher Caynes | 1 | 11 | | Wido Cross | 0 | 9 | 2 |
| william northiner | 0 | 11 | | Mr Thorlton | 1 | 8 | |
| allon dyke for willets | 1 | 9 | | william stephens | 0 | 1 | |
| Mr Cumpton | 0 | 10 | 2 | Mr willsheer | 0 | 9 | |
| Joseph Edwards | 0 | 10 | 2 | Ms Lane | 1 | 1 | |
| old mrs mitchell | 0 | 7 | 2 | Mr whitacher | 0 | 10 | |
| mrs mitchell | 2 | 1 | 4 | John Holler | 0 | 3 | c |
| widw Raynel | 0 | 4 | 2 | Esua Lush | 0 | 6 | 2 |
| william mitchell | 0 | 8 | | Cylges | 0 | 1 | i |
| allen dyke | 0 | 1 | | Mr Rowes | 0 | 3 | |
| Richart pope | 0 | 10 | | Mr willises | 1 | 9 | |
| abel pope | 0 | 4 | | John Caynes | 0 | 2 | |
| Mr Huelet | 2 | 1 | | Mr Brankers | 0 | 7 | i |
| Mr Chafil | 0 | 6 | 2 | Mr Creeds | 1 | 3 | |
| Mr Thomas muston | 0 | 11 | 4 | Corbing mill | 1 | 3 | |
| abolsbury pasindgs | 1 | 0 | | Bealy hayes | 0 | 6 | i |
| Breathos Ground | 0 | 2 | 2 | Mr Cleues | 0 | 11 | |
| Robert shitler | 0 | 3 | | Mr Elsworth | 0 | 4 | |
| Laurenes mitchell | 0 | 4 | 2 | Bucklands | 0 | 3 | |
| abolsbery Land | | | | Ockford Lands | 0 | 2 | |
| Joseph small | 0 | 1 | 2 | Mr Brient | 0 | 2 | i |
| Parish ground | 0 | 6 | | Mr Brient | 0 | 1 | i |
| Smart for Bayntons | 0 | 6 | | wido Someny | 0 | 2 | i |
| John Chapman | 0 | 1 | | John Gilbord | 0 | 2 | i |
| william northouer | 0 | 3 | | william Langhorn | 1 | 3 | i |
| Joseph Sunford | 0 | 0 | 2 | | | | |
| Joseph still | 0 | 1 | 2 | | | | |
| Charles Lydford | 0 | 1 | | | | | |
| | 2 | 2 | 6 | | 1 | 17 | 4 | 2 |
| | | | | | 3 | 19 | 10 | i |

4. Finding potential manuscript sources for ancestors' individual situations.

5. Using manuscript sources for 'active' background purposes.

To consider these in detail:

*1. Re-examining genealogical sources* The difference between genealogical and family history research is similar to that between the archaeology of the early nineteenth century and that of today. The early archaeologist was what we now look upon as a mere antiquary. If he was fortunate enough to dig up, say, an Anglo-Saxon gold torque, he would shovel the earth back and carry away his prize rejoicing. But today, archaeology, the study of non-documentary evidence of the human past, has become scientific. A single find, such as the torque, would be regarded as a potential clue to so much more. It would have to be considered in relation to the depth of earth at which it lay, to variations in the surrounding soil, the pattern of the fields above, existing knowledge of the locality's history and other related items of evidence, all of which taken together might lead to excavation of the whole site and the discovery of an early human settlement, causing a revision of the history of the surrounding area.

In family history the same research principles apply. When an ancestor's name is discovered in a document, its 'site' needs to be examined and considered for what it shows. For instance, his name in a local directory can reveal much more than his mere existence at a certain place and date. If the other residents of the street are seen to be tradesmen and craftsmen, they show he was living in a certain social milieu; but if they were Dr Watson and Colonel Newcome, he was in a different set; and residences in the street of Lady Bracknell and the Ruritanian Ambassador would be signs of yet another. For family history purposes, the wording surrounding a mention of an ancestor should be transcribed for what it may eventually reveal, either by itself or in connection with other discoveries. Personally, I note the names and occupations of every householder listed in an ancestor's street. In addition to what pointers such occupations and titles give to the economic and social status of the ancestor's environment, one or more of the householders may well turn up again and be revealed as associated with the family in some interesting connection, giving relevance to the fact that he was also a close neighbour, a circumstance that has happened in my history more than once.

*2. Unused genealogical sources* What these are will differ as between one genealogist and another. Only civil registration certificates of births,

*An ancestor named in this list of church ratepayers is shown among his neighbours, and the relative value of the property he occupied is thus revealed by the amount he paid, shown here in shillings, pence and farthings.*

# Militia List.

A true list of all Persons usually, and at this time, dwelling within the Parish of St James; in the Town and County of the Town of Poole, in the County of Dorset, between the Ages of Eighteen and Forty-five Years; distinguishing their Ranks and Occupations, Family, Size, Exemptions and Infirmities. — Dated the 8th day of Nov. 1798. —

| Names | Ranks & Occupations | Family — Wife | Children | Size — Feet | Inches | Exemptions and Infirmities |
|---|---|---|---|---|---|---|
| Richard ——— | Victualler | wife | 4 | 5 | 6 | |
| George Knight Sen. | — | — | 1 | 5 | 9 | |
| Jos. Mogg Jun. | Ropemaker | W | 2 | 5 | 5 | |
| Jos. Mogg | Ropemaker | | | 5 | 5 | in Association |
| ——— | | | | 5 | 7 | Apprentice VA |
| Wm ——— | Cordwainer | W | | 6 | 0 | Volunteer VA |
| John Martin | Ropemaker | W | | 5 | 6 | |
| Wm Rowe | Mariner | W | 3 | 5 | 10 | in Association |
| Wm Rogers | Mariner | | | 5 | 5 | Volunteer B |
| George Marshman | Labourer | W | | 5 | 8 | Pauper |
| David Moore | Labourer | | | 5 | 10 | Volunteer VA |
| Andrew Dewey | Higgler | W | 3 | 5 | 9 | |
| George Baker | ——— | | | 5 | 5 | Volunteer |
| Will West | Cordwainer | | | 5 | 10 | Under Size |
| John Hutchins | Blacksmith | Ap | 3 | 5 | 5 | Volunteer B |
| James ——— | Painter | W | 4 | 5 | 5 | in Association |
| Wm Lewis | Joiner | W | 2 | 5 | 6 | |
| Geo Brown | Coal Meter | W | | 5 | 5 | Pauper |
| James ——— | Breechesmaker | W | | 5 | 10 | Under Size |

| Names | Ranks & Occupations | Family — Wife | Children | Size — Feet | Inches | Exemptions and Infirmities |
|---|---|---|---|---|---|---|
| John Longman | Carpenter | wife | 3 | 5 | 0 | Volunteer VA |
| Richard ——— | | Do | 6 | 5 | 7 | in Association |
| John ——— Manufacr | | W | 2 | 5 | 0 | |
| ——— | | | | 5 | 5 | Volunteer VA |
| John Davis | Labourer | W | 1 | 5 | 6 | |
| Wm Randall | Joiner | W | 6 | 5 | 4 | Volunteer VA |
| Andrew Wise | Taylor | | | 5 | 9 | |
| John Barnes | Labourer | | | 5 | 4 | Parish Cavalry |
| James ——— | Cordwainer | | | 5 | 4 | Apprentice |
| Geo ——— | Labourer | | | 5 | 6 | Lind by Substitute |
| James Bull | Cordwainer | W | 2 | 5 | 6 | Volunteer VA |
| John ——— | Do | | | 5 | 7 | Do B |
| ——— | | W | 3 | 5 | 7 | Apprentice |
| Lewis Chappell | Cordwainer | | | 5 | 5 | Do |
| Sepht Moneham | Do | | | 5 | 5 | Volunteer VA |
| Wm Pike | Do | | | 5 | 7 | |
| Henry Baker | Butcher | | | 5 | 6 | |
| James ——— | | W | | 5 | | in Association |

deaths and marriages, census returns, parish registers, bishops' transcripts and wills can be safely taken as searched. Few genealogists will have covered all the other extant records of even their local areas. Among these I include the parish's vestry minutes, the accounts of churchwardens, constables and surveyors of the highways, settlement papers, monumental inscriptions, manor court records, estate accounts, borough ward records, church terriers, the local school's attendance lists and governors' minutes, poor apprentice bindings and local newspapers. Then there are the local sections of the records of wider areas or jurisdictions: census returns, directories, lay subsidy, hearth and poll tax lists, Protestation Oath returns, freeholders' lists, poll books, certificates of residence, muster certificates, tithe and enclosure awards, and inheritance taxes. Then on to individual entries in records of still wider jurisdiction, to search which one is dependent on catalogues or indexes. Among these I include the records of urban corporations, livery companies, Quarter Sessions, assizes, equity courts, ecclesiastical courts and visitations, inventories, newspapers, state papers, close and patent rolls, and inquisitions post mortem; but all these are only examples, there is no possibility of any complete list.

*3. Reading published histories for contexts and backgrounds* The character-istics that distinguish a family history from a family tree written out in narrative form are the setting of the characters in their social scene, the relating of their experiences and, as far as possible, the reasons for their actions and situations. Every background and context in which they are found, both long-term ones, such as their homes, neighbourhoods and occupations, and short-term single actions and events, need to be researched independently of the documents in which the ancestors themselves have been found. In fact, background and context research constitutes as large a part of the total family history task as discovering mentions of the family members, and can be every bit as fascinating.

Published historical works on subjects relating to the family's past should always be looked out for on public library shelves and in bibliographies, book reviews and historical journals. They should be studied for two separate purposes, one of which we will consider under the next heading. First, for any light the author's text can throw on the family's social setting: occupational, domestic, local (geographical), communal (jurisdictional), and national. All potentially useful passages should be transcribed for eventual transformation into narrative

*In the early days of the Napoleonic Wars, expectation of invasion led to the formation of numerous militia units. At a county record office a muster roll such as this is particularly revealing about the menfolk of the district, showing their height, infirmities, status, occupation and family.*

background material. The possibility of finding even foreground material cannot be entirely ruled out. Although it is usually too much to expect the book to mention the ancestor himself, occasionally it will mention a group to which he belonged. For instance, a history of the battles of World War I is likely to mention the battalion in which your ancestor served.

In addition to searching the works of modern historians for relevant background information, I am strongly drawn to those that were published shortly after the events they describe. This is because I want to know how those events were thought of, however mistakenly, by people at the time, and also to pick up minor but humanly illustrative details not worth mention in later assessments of the general situation. For access to these old books, a pass to the British Library reading room at the British Museum, or to one of the other great libraries, is pretty well essential.

The modern books and articles that you read for this purpose will also provide your best pointers to further coverage of the same and allied subjects. These will be shown in a bibliography at the end, listing the published works the author has consulted; and many of these will also be worth your perusal.

*4. Wider manuscript research* Historical material obtained from the text and bibliography of a published work does not constitute all the useful information they contain. The author will also have listed, usually under the heading *References*, the original manuscript sources for his statements and conclusions. These open for the family historian a door to records beyond the genealogical ranges listed above, to ones that relate specifically to situations in which the ancestor has been found and which are the cause of reading the background history. The fact that the author has already drawn upon these manuscript sources does not mean that there will be nothing new for you to find in them; he has extracted only what he needed for his own particular purposes. By making use of such resources, the amateur family historian advances his researches on the backs, as it were, of professional historians.

*5. Use of manuscript sources for backgrounds and contexts* When I first set out on my researches, I expected to derive all my background material from secondary sources, published histories of one kind and another. I felt that, with original research into my family's activities taking up so much time, I could hardly expect myself to research contemporary manuscript sources for their backgrounds as well; and anyway, with so many national, local and other histories already in print, surely that would not be necessary. That comfortable but immature view of the task ahead soon went by the board.

Published histories will of course be major sources, but some backgrounds stand so close to an ancestor that tiny items, of no concern to historians working on larger subjects, may well have been of important relevance to him; so, for these, research into the original records can sometimes provide answers not to be found in published works. For instance, although I had read printed histories of the Merchant Taylors Company, compiled from the records of that organisation, and had found a great deal of usable material, I had found nothing to throw any light upon one point that intrigued me: why in 1668 my ancestor had been made a liveryman at the early age of twenty-six, although his father had always been one of the majority of members who remained rank and file members. However, when I progressed from reading the published history of the Company to searching the actual *Minute Books of the Court of Assistants*, it was there that I found the reason for the young man's early admission. The Company was facing a financial emergency. Its revenues had been greatly reduced by the Fire of London, the cost of restoring Merchant Taylors' Hall was considerable, and now one of the Company's members had landed it in enormous expense by getting elected Lord Mayor. As one measure to improve their cash flow, the Court of Assistants decided to appoint an exceptionally large number of freemen to the livery for the sake of their admission fees. So young William Fitzhugh was one of twenty-nine freemen whose £25 entry fee helped to defray the cost of that year's Lord Mayor's Show and Banquet.

By and large, a foreground piece of information, by which I mean the mention of a member of the family or a group to which he belonged, tells *What happened* and *When*. It nearly always leaves the *How* and the *Why* to be searched for in background sources. And when you come to write up your family history, you will often find that the How and Why of an episode will fill more page space than the What and When; and only through the former pair will the latter become understandable and interesting. So it is your background discoveries that will give your finished volume its conviction and readability — and also its bulk.

When I found the multifarious requirements of research exceeding the capacity of my memory, I designed a form to act as a combined rapid-reference record of all searches needing to be made and already made; and I had a stock of a dozen photocopies of it run off (as overleaf). In use, each one is headed with the name of a record repository or library, e.g. Public Record Office, Chancery Lane, Guildhall Library, British Library, Greater London Record Office, Bucks Record Office, etc. As each search idea occurs to me I enter it on the appropriate sheet in column 1 or columns 1 and 2. If there is no urgency, I put off my visit to any given repository until I have three or four queries calling for my attention there.

## Research

When on the spot, I enter up columns 3 and 4, and before I come away column 5 with my Results. For these, I have brief codes: *O.K., N.G. Cont[inued] from p..., Rec[ord] in use, Rec not there*, and so on. In the case of the last three, I enter the requirement again in columns 1, 2 and 3 for a future visit. I keep all the forms and their continuation sheets together in a loose-leaf binder in alphabetical order of repositories. Separately I keep a blank form from which to make further photocopies. These ready-reference sheets I find invaluable to remind me quickly of searches made and needing to be made.

Having made a find and transcribed it in pencil, the researcher then has to file it for eventual use when writing his history, a subject requiring our next consideration.

| Information Sought | Title of Record | Call Mark | Date Searched | Result |
|---|---|---|---|---|
| Will of John Fitzhugh, 1607 | P.C.C. Will | PROB.11/110 | | OK |
| Progress of Ward - Fitzhugh suit | Chancery Decrees & Orders | C.33/848 | | OK |
| Ditto | Ditto | C.33/849 | | OK |
| Ditto | Ditto | C.33/861 | | OK |
| Any Fitzhugh military mention | Muster Rolls, 1644-51 | SP.28/120 | | unindexed. No search |
| Stratton - Frye Correspondence | Chan. Masters Exhibits | C.113/12 | | OK |
| Warton - Fitzhugh suit, c.1545 | Court of Requests | REQ/2/10/252 | | OK |
| Henry Lane guardianship | Close Roll | C.54/11225 | | OK |
| Did Wm. Fitzhugh call at Florence 1752 | Tuscany, Minister Misc 1744-71 | SP.105/302 | | N G. |
| Anything re Wm Fitzhugh & Aleppo | Levant Co. Aleppo. Letter Book | SP.110/29 | | OK |
| Information re St Vincent, c.1766 | Acts of Privy Council, Col. Series Vol 5 | open shelf | | OK. |
| | | | | |
| | | | | |
| | | | | |
| | | | | |
| | | | | |
| | | | | |
| | | | | |
| | | | | |

Public Record Office, Chancery Lane

*The author's rapid-reference record of searches made.*

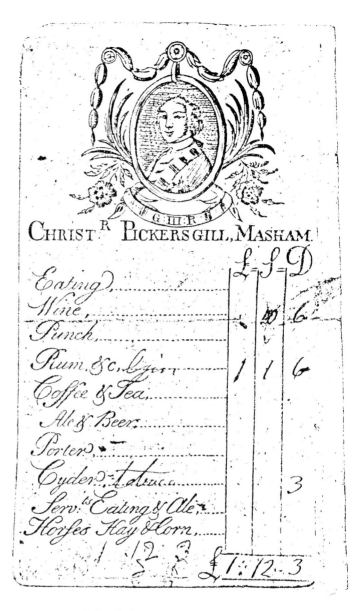

*An interesting find from a store of family papers, this tavern bill reveals how much John Mumforth, parish constable of Exelby, North Yorkshire, spent on gin at nearby Masham in 1797.*

# 4
# Record keeping

On two occasions, many years ago now, I had the melancholy duty of sorting through the papers of someone recently deceased. Each time, I came upon a store of family memorabilia that was a pathetic pile of miscellanea: loose sheets of family trees, news cuttings, letters, notes, some on large sheets, some on small, some folded one way, some another, studio photographs and snapshots without identifying names; and the whole pile looking, to any less sympathetic executor, perfect dustbin material. The experience made up my mind for me that when I died my collection of family records should survive me in all the dignity of an heirloom.

## Record keeping

Many genealogical manuals offer advice on the best way to keep order among the transcripts and photocopies that accumulate in the course of research. They advise keeping all the census returns in one file, wills in another, parish register entries in a third, etc. To me, that is like recovering the skeletons of one's ancestors and storing all their tibias together in one box, femurs in another, and so on. It is an analytical system, taking constituent pieces apart, and will probably do very well if your aims are purely genealogical, but if a family history is your aim you need a synthetical system, bringing constituent parts together and in their proper order. And 'proper' means where you can most effectively refer to them while working. When writing a narrative, what you will constantly be needing to know is: What happened next? So your only practical filing system will be chronological.

With both dignity and chronology in mind, I invested in an expensive binder of the kind that, though technically loose-leaf in the sense that new sheets can be inserted in any order, grips the sheets firmly, and holds 500 of them. It was of the type that commercial companies use for business records. I then had the most daunting task of typing onto its pages all the handwritten transcripts I had made during the previous twenty years. I therefore strongly recommend all who aim eventually at writing a narrative history to transfer to a chronological record system at the earliest possible moment. Family history writing on any respectable scale is impossible without it.

Now, thirty-odd years later, a long space on my bookshelves is occupied by twenty of those binders containing thousands of Family Transcripts. I still worry about their future beyond my grave. Will either of my sons really spare house-room for such a number, and if not, would even the Society of Genealogists welcome the offer of them? All the more necessary is the completion of my narrative history and its distribution in numerous copies.

Chronological record keeping necessarily requires that the documentary evidence of family events, most of which will have been first transcribed at a record office in pencil, must then be retranscribed, preferably by typewriter or word processor, on to a separate sheet of paper for each day on which an event occurred; and if an event continues for several days, it must be given a separate sheet for each day. Likewise, to enable the sheets to be kept in chronological order, they must be dated. I type the date in the top right-hand corner of the sheet thus:

1763<br>
SEP<br>
17<br>
SAT

The date must, of course, be that of the family event, not that of the record, unless of course the two are the same. The day of the week can be drawn from a Perpetual Calendar, such as is shown in my *Dictionary of Genealogy*. If the record extends over more than both sides of a sheet, as it often does, especially with background material, I head the continuation sheet: '[CONTINUATION OF 17 SEPTEMBER 1763]'; and, if necessary: [2ND CONTINUATION OF 17 SEPTEMBER 1763].

Having dated the sheet, the document to be typed on to it must be identified by its title, call number and whereabouts. I do this in capital letters. If the source is a printed book, its author and date of edition must be shown. Sometimes a passage that you transcribe from a printed history book will be a quotation from an original manuscript. In such cases, both the title of the book and that of the quoted document must be shown, with the former as your main heading.

The record itself then follows, copied from your pencilled transcript. Sometimes you will have transcribed only part of a document, omitting an irrelevant section or sections at the beginning, middle or end. Such omissions made by your own decision must be indicated. I do this by three dashes (- - -). The way such omissions are indicated in a printed book when quoting from some other source is usually by three dots (. . .). When transcribing such a text, copy the dots as shown in print. Then, in your volumes of transcripts, the use of dashes will show clearly that you yourself have made the omissions, and dots will indicate that the omissions occurred in your printed source. In either case you may later decide you need to go back to the original manuscript to make a fuller transcript.

Sometimes an original document will describe events that happened on a number of different non-consecutive dates. An example of this is the Chancery suit on pages 120-22, in which the Bill of Complaint and the Answer mentioned events spreading over many years. To maintain your chronological arrangement of events, you will need to split such a text up under the different dates. For ease of later reference, you should begin each section after the first with 'Continued from' and the date of the previous section; and end each section except the last with 'Continued on' followed by the date of the next section. These words, being additions of your own, should be typed in square brackets.

Often the exact date of an incident will not be indicated. For instance, all you will have for an address extracted from a local directory is the year shown on the title page. In such cases, I date my sheet with just the year and insert it into my Family Transcript Binder at the beginning of that year (actually, in the case of directories, the information may really only be true for the preceding year). Sometimes a year and month are indicated, but no day. In such a case I date the sheet with just that information and insert it at the beginning of the appropriate month.

For periods earlier than the change of the calendar in 1752, I show the year on all incidents between the 1st January and 24th March as (e.g.) 1689/90. Sometimes, although an exact date is not shown, one can deduce it approximately from other evidence. In that case I show the day of the month as (e.g.) *c.* 17th, and omit the weekday.

I recommend the underlining in red ink of the names of all members of your own family, by birth or marriage. That will greatly speed the finding of a name when you are flicking through the pages later on. I also underline the names of my ancestresses' relations in blue, and sisters' husbands and their relations in green. Treated in that way they all show up on the pages at a glance. I even award such people their coloured underlinings before they have earned them by marriage. For instance, a man who was my ancestor's business partner in Canton, China, throughout the 1780s retired home to England and married the ancestor's sister. I have underlined him in green ink from the time he was first mentioned in Canton. As a further visual aid, I type the names of all actual ancestors and ancestresses, including ancestresses' parents, in capitals, which helps to distinguish them from identically named siblings.

I do make one exception to my principle of a separate sheet, or sheets, for each day on which an event occurred. When my source document is a diary or a ship's journal, or army war diary, covering every day of an extended period, I enter as many days on one sheet as there is room for on both sides, but only those within the same calendar month, and I page-number it as (e.g.):

1857

OCT

1-15

I do this solely to prevent the number of my Family Transcript volumes becoming astronomical. There is an occasional disadvantage attached to it, but not serious enough to outweigh the great saving in bulk. During these continuous stretches of daily events, another event or additional evidence for one of the days is quite likely to occur. If, in the above example, a later incident were found for the 10th October, the sheet would have to be retyped on three sheets page-numbered 1857/OCT/1-9, 1857/OCT/10 (carrying the day's diary entry plus the new evidence), and 1857/OCT/11-15; and that is a bit tiresome.

I have had occasion to transcribe a number of eighteenth-century ships' logbooks and journals (the joint title indicates that they contain two types of information). If the member of my family sailing in the vessel was one of the ship's crew, I have transcribed the whole journal (of incidents other than logbook navigational technicalities), because in a ship of only a few hundred tons pretty well everything that happened affected every one of the crew. But if the Fitzhugh on board was a passenger, I have transcribed only incidents likely to have been of concern to him.

A transcribed extract from some documents, e.g. parish registers, will consist of no more than a dozen words; so you may expect your sheets of Family Transcripts to show a lot of unoccupied white space. There certainly will be some like that, but not nearly as many as you expect. For writing a family history, documentary mentions of members of the family are only one of two essential requirements. The other, the one so often ignored by authors of 'family histories', comprises all the contexts (the backgrounds) into which such a narrative has to place the members of the family if it is to be in any way worthy of the name of history.

The term 'background material' here includes every item of evidence that adds to your knowledge of your ancestors' lives and circumstances. What these items are likely to be has been mentioned in the chapter on Research, and will be discussed in detail in the chapters that follow. All that concerns us here are the entries for them in your Family Transcript volumes, entries that will not only fill a great deal of the blank space below your foreground entries, but will often require continuation sheets.

Each transcript of background material should be as carefully attributed to its source as those of mentions of your family, i.e. by the title of the manuscript or printed book. If ever a statement in your history is challenged by a reader, you will then be able to quote your authority. Do not necessarily confine yourself to entering only one source of information on each subject. One nineteenth-century guide book on a locality may well supplement another, or perhaps contradict it.

Background material should always be entered on the Family Transcript sheet to which it is most relevant, so that when you come to write up your narrative it will come to your attention just when you need it. For instance, a sheet bearing an extract from a Poll Book showing how your ancestor voted in a parliamentary election will be the proper sheet on which to add any background information from other sources about the election itself or the policies of the candidates your ancestor favoured. Background material is often of long-term application, such as the description of a village in which your ancestor lived. Ideally, this should go on the sheet containing the first evidence of his presence there. Similarly, on the page bearing the first mention of the young woman who is to become your ancestress, enter all you know about her and her family background (birth, parentage, father's occupation, etc.); and it is useful to illustrate it with a short family tree showing her parents and siblings.

Sometimes you will find a piece of background material you cannot attach to any one particular mention of your family. In 1603 the Privy Council received a report that plague had broken out in the City of London, 'and especially in Southwark - - - and it is feared that next year it will be very contagious'. A member of my family, John Fitzhugh, was living in Southwark at that time, so I thought this well worth transcribing; but as I had no mention of him for either that year or the next, my note of the plague was given a sheet to itself dated 1603. Had some incident involving John in the same year turned up later, I would have added it on the same sheet and given it its exact date.

When typing an entry into your Family Transcript volume, you sometimes need to insert a word or phrase of your own. This should be done in square brackets to distinguish it from any parenthesis in the original, which should be enclosed in the usual curved brackets. For example, on page 146, in my newscutting about the first crossing of the Solent by steamboat, I have inserted two words to make the reporter's meaning clear to present-day readers. Sometimes the original text contains an obvious mistake or other mis-statement, and this it is customary to highlight by the insertion of [*sic*]. If a word has been inadvertently omitted, the omission can be rectified in square brackets. If I am not sure that I have read a word correctly, I add [*?*], and if I cannot read it at all, I replace it with [*illeg. word*].

On the sample Family Transcript shown on page 33, some of these points are illustrated. In the top left-hand corner I have shown the current monarch. This is just an optional extra. For me, the reign is more evocative of mental pictures than the Anno Domini date.

When I was young and starting my ancestral quest, 'history' ended when I was born. Anything after that date lay outside the sphere of my researches. But when war broke out in 1939 I could not but recognise that my family stood on the brink of 'History' in a very big way. My brother and I were both of military age, and my sister was living in eastern Germany, wife of a charming fellow who was now one of our enemy. I decided that our family's experiences must be recorded. My first idea was to keep a diary, but I remembered that in World War I soldiers had been forbidden to carry diaries on active service in case they were captured and valuable information fell into enemy hands. So I decided to keep every

*This Family History Transcript sheet for the 9th February, 1808, shows 'foreground information' — an 11-year-old boy joining the navy as midshipman — supplemented by three items of 'background material' — the whereabouts of his ship, an explanation of his being under age, and the character of his captain.*

## THE MUSTER BOOK OF H.M.S. TARTAR, P.R.O. ADM.37/1839

| Complement | Ship's Company | Volunteers & Boys | Marines | Supernumeraries |
|---|---|---|---|---|
| 254 | 46 | 18 | 29 | 17 |

Thos. Sykes, 1st Lieut; H. Caight, 2nd Lieut; George Anson Byron, 3rd Lieut; John Ross, Purser.

### Volunteers 1th Class

| | |
|---|---|
| Year: | 1808 |
| Appearance: | Feby 9th. |
| Whether Prest or not: | Volunteer. |
| Where Born: | London. |
| Age at entry: | 13 [sic, really 11.] |
| Men's Names: | Henry Fitzhugh. |
| No. & Letter of Ticket: | ND 902. |
| D, DD or R: | DD. |
| Two Months' Advance: | 1-7-8 |

## LOG OF THE PROCEEDINGS OF H.M.S. TARTAR, KEPT BY G.E.B. BETTESWORTH, ESQR, CAPTAIN. P.R.O, ADM. 51/1792

Fevruary 1808, Tuesday 9th: [Lashed alongside the 'Janus' hulk since 5th Feb.] A.M. Moderate and Clear. Employed as necessary. Riggers rattling down the rigging. P.M. Cloudy with rain. Employed as most necessary, wash'd decks and Muster'd ship's company per ship's books.

## A SOCIAL HISTORY OF THE NAVY, 1793-1815, BY MICHAEL LEWIS (1960)

Two rules - - - governed the rating [of midshipmen] - - -. First, no one could receive it until he had been at sea for two years; and, second, he was not allowed to begin his two-year qualifying period - not allowed at sea at all - until he was 13 years old or, if a naval officer's son, 11 years' old.

So much for the rules. But our Table shows some 366 officers who allege that it was as midshipmen that they first went to sea. - - - What they were doing was regulation dodging; and solely with a view to becoming Lieutenants as early as possible - - -.

First, one could break the entry-age regulation and send a lad to sea before he was 13 (or 11 if a naval officer's son). - - - To quote but three examples - - - Nelson went to sea at 12, Collingwood and Cornwallis at 11; and their fathers were none of them naval officers.

## DICTIONARY OF NATIONAL BIOGRAPHY

Bettesworth, George Edmund Byron

[Abstract: George E.B. Bettesworth mar. Hannah Althea,
2nd dau. of 1st Earl Grey.
m. at St George's, Han. Sq,
London, 24.9.1807.]

- - - (1805) received a post-captain's commission. Lord Byron, in October 1807, wrote: 'Next January - - - I am going to sea for four or five months with my cousin, Captain Bettesworth, who commands the Tartar, the finest frigate in the navy - - -. We are going probably to the Mediterranean or to the West Indies, or to the devil; and if there is a possibility of taking me to the latter, Bettesworth will do it, for he has received four-and-twenty wounds in different places, and at this moment possesses a letter from the late Lord Nelson stating that Bettesworth is the only officer in the navy who had more wlunds than himself.' The promised voyage never took place.

## SHIPS OF THE ROYAL NAVY, BY J.J. COLLEDGE (1969)

Tartar: 5th rate 32, 885 bm, 142 x 37½ ft. Brindley, Frindsbury 27.6.1801. Wrecked 18.8.1811 in the Baltic.

letter written to me by any member of the family, and arranged for my wife to keep my letters to her. Looking back on them all now (retyped into my Family Transcripts), I realise how greatly their diverse reflections of so many different aspects of the war transcend in interest any possible diary of my personal experiences and impressions. Letters from my brother fighting across North Africa to Tangier, where he saw our brother-in-law brought in a prisoner-of-war, 25-word communications from my sister in Germany via the Swiss Red Cross, her flight before the advancing Red Army, weekly correspondence from my parents in the north of England, news of my wife coping with rations, two small children and Land Army welfare work, my own letters of life in the RAF, and finally my parents' agonised refusal to accept that my brother was 'missing, reported killed' in Normandy a week after D Day.

My typed transcripts of this family war correspondence brought home to me how truly the present is also history. Since then I have filled more binders with transcripts of Contemporary Family History consisting of records about my parents' and my own generation, all from originals in my personal possession. Since it was never my plan to include autobiography in my family history, I was slow to undertake any research into contemporary records housed elsewhere. This omission I have recently been rectifying with investigation into the experiences of my father and his brothers in World War I, an event that younger family researchers will have less difficulty in recognising as history.

As we family historians feel in duty bound not to allow our ancestors to sink into oblivion, we owe it to our descendants not to allow ourselves to become a gap in their history.

# 5

# The ancestor as private person

We will now run through ancestral life at all its stages, starting even before the muling and puking, and ending after the slippers have finally been laid aside. At each period, there may be more for a historian to find and write about than the documents he has found tell him in so many words.

To a genealogist, the lives of Victorian ancestors began with their births as recorded in the General Register; and in earlier times only with their baptisms. But birth is the climax of a process; and the preceding pregnancy may sometimes be a condition worth narrative attention. An example that I have in mind from my own family was when the Civil War had just broken out and London was the first target of the King's forces. The Roundhead Fitzhughs lived at the first house on Old London Bridge from the Southwark side, which, being the only river crossing, was the obvious point for any royalist attack from the south. Worse, they were outside the city's defences, because the bridge's portcullised gatehouse and drawbridge stood between them and the north bank. The threat of attack and their exposure to it, worrying in themselves, must have been all the more stressful for my ancestress Mary Fitzhugh, who was eight months pregnant. As events turned out, the advancing Cavalier army got no further than the outer western suburbs of London, and retreated without mounting a siege, but the fact that the circumstances of Mary's pregnancy and fear of flight from home were unrecorded could result in the historian's missing a time of family stress and a link with national events that combined to provide an excellent narrative opportunity.

## Birth

Although before 1st July 1837 the earliest recorded sign of life in an ancestor was usually the entry of his or her baptism in a parish register, some parsons or parish clerks did sometimes add dates of actual birth or provided the same information by saying how old the child was at baptism. Of this latter type of entry it must be remembered that until well into the nineteenth century, periods of time, when reckoned in smaller

George Woolley was bp? May 1861

Rose - Anna Woolley was Born July-16-1863-

3

} Thomas William. Woolley 1835
  Born at Netherbury July 7th 1835

} Harriet Woolley
  Born November 21st {1833} 1833

Married 11 1858 at Netherbury.

—: Their Children —

Ellen. Woolley        Born   Aug 21st 1859
                      Christ.  Sep      1859
                      Died   Sep 21st   1869

George Woolley        Born   May 8th  1861
                      Bap    June     1861
                      Died   Sep 3rd  1869

Rosalie Anna          Born   July 16th 1863
  Woolley             Bap    Aug      1863
                      Died   Sep 2nd  1864

Frederick Woolley     Born   March 3rd 1865
                      Bapt   April     1865
                      Died   May 2nd   1866

Elizabeth Woolley Born July 26th 1867
                      Bap    Sp       1867
                      Died   Sep 17th 1869

Mary Anne.            Born   May 17th 1869
                      Bap    June     1869
                      Confirmed oct 24th 1883

*Victorian married couples often entered important family dates on a blank page in their bible. If all four death certificates issued in September 1869 show a common illness, the parish register and local newspaper may reveal the ravages of an epidemic.*

units such as the days of a month or years of a century, were counted from the first unit, instead of from its completion as we do now. Because of this, a baby was thought to be one day, or even one year, old directly it was born; and George III's Golden Jubilee celebrations started on the very first day of his fiftieth year on the throne. So if an early baptismal entry mentions that the child was eleven days old, it means that he or she was ten days old by modern computation.

Another thing to bear in mind about a birth is that it cannot always be safely assumed to have happened a few days or weeks before the christening. Infant baptism, though expected by the Church of England, was not invariable in practice. There were parents whom the Church's influence did not fully reach. Their children might go unbaptised for years. Sometimes it was the zeal of a new incumbent, paying his initial visits around the parish and finding a couple with an unchristened child, that caused it to be admitted into the Church several years late. If there were a number of little heathens in the family, they might then be baptised together in a batch. I have read in a family history of a boy, registered at baptism as illegitimate, who, according to the historian, married at the age of fourteen a woman in her twenties. A far more likely interpretation of the evidence would be that he had not been baptised as an infant.

*This parish register page from 1748 shows the baptism and burial of an illegitimate infant, followed in ten days by the marriage of the mother. Such entries cause speculation. Was it a knobstick wedding? The Vestry Minutes may mention the churchwardens' intervention.*

Ten or a dozen births in a family were not uncommon even into the nineteenth century, and in families of that size the baptisms sometimes followed one another at surprisingly brief intervals. These indicate that the mother, by not breast-feeding a child, had curtailed the lactation period during which she could not conceive again. Many working-class women lost their children after a few weeks or months of life, and so were available to be employed as wet-nurses for the infants of mothers with a number of other children on their hands. This had the unintended effect of bringing forward the employing mother's liability to conceive again. Occasionally the fact that a child was put out to nurse is documented, but this usually occurs only when it dies in infancy and the burial register describes it as a nurse-child. In my family, William Fitzhugh, a third child, was baptised on 30th October 1717, only eleven months after his next elder brother, who therefore must have been a nurse-child; and then, when William himself died in infancy, the register of St John's, Hackney read:

> William Fitzhugh, a nurse-child, was buried on the 18th day of July 1718

A fifth child, Richard, was baptised in February 1720, only fourteen months after his sister. Eight months later he died, and the register of St John's recorded:

> Richard Fitzhugh, a nurse-child, was carried away on the 6th day of October 1720

And next day's entry in the register of St Peter's Cornhill, where the family lived, read:

> 1720 October 7. Richard Fitzhugh buried: South Chapel

Every discovered incident in a family's history should if possible be set within its background. The newborn baby's home context will be discussed in another chapter, but outdoors, at an ancestor's birth and any other time, there was always the English weather. A casual mention of rain or sunshine conveys a sense of intimacy with the situation. One good source of meteorological information for a particular place — our weather being extremely local — is private diaries, many of which have been published, while others survive in manuscript in record offices and

*Large families of short-lived children were once the rule for all classes of the community, but high child mortality continued longer among the working classes. The photograph shows young children, in a Glasgow slum, many of whom may never have seen adulthood.*

private collections. Anyone with ancestors living near Dorothy Wordsworth will have plenty of meteorological background to draw upon. I have occasionally been lucky in this respect, and never more so than at the baptism of William Fitzhugh on Old London Bridge at the beginning of January 1684 — which is why I am mentioning the weather at this particular point. He came into the world during one of the coldest spells the capital had ever experienced; and there on the spot, among many others who described the famous scene, was the diarist John Evelyn, who wrote:

> *January the 9th* I went across the Thames upon the ice, which was now become so incredibly thick as to bear not only whole streets of booths, in which they roasted meat and had divers shops of wares as in a town, but also coaches and carts and horses, which passed over. ...

And when, in the same bleak month of the year 1800, Thomas Fitzhugh died in London, my account of the sad event will include the sympathetic reaction of the heavens. The issue of the *Evening Mail* that announced his death also reported:

> From the rain, snow and hail that fell on Wednesday night and Thursday morning, the streets of London were never known more slippery; several accidents happened.

However, with death we are getting a long way ahead of schedule.

## Religion

In past centuries religion, and consequently the influence of the Church authorities, permeated most aspects of social life. Did the ancestor remain faithful to the tenets in which his parents brought him up, or did he undergo the stresses of doubt and conversion to another denomination? If, after being himself christened as a member of the Church of England, he had his children baptised in a non-conformist chapel, what was it that brought about that change? A question that a family historian must be asking himself at all changes, and looking for the answer. Was it perhaps the influence of his wife? To find out, a search of the earlier records of the chapel should be made for signs of her and/or her parents as members of that congregation. The fact that the couple were married in a Church of England church was, between 1754 and 1837, no indication of their adherence to its tenets, because no one except Quakers and Jews were given any option in the matter. Also, in early non-conformist days, the fact

| | | | |
|---|---|---|---|
| | | **Wymondham Society** | |
| | | **List of Members Dec 1876** | |
| | 1 | George Lane | Middleton St |
| | 2 | John R Smith | Town Green |
| | 3 | Charles Higgins | do |
| D | 4 | William Minns | Norwich Road |
| | 5 | Mary Woodbine | Kidds Moor |
| | 6 | Charlotte Lane | Middleton St |
| | 7 | George Howes | People St |
| | 8 | Mahala Howes | do |
| | 9 | Elizabeth Thurston | Kidds Moor |
| D | 10 | Ann Smith | The Lizard |
| | 11 | Elizth Hipperson | Fairland St |
| D | 12 | Martha Minns | Fairland used with her sister Fuller |
| D | 13 | James Knivett | |
| L | 14 | Ellen Knivett | |
| | 15 | Amelia Elsey | Railway Road |
| | 16 | Jabez Thoower | Middleton St |
| | 17 | Robert Swatman | Norwich Rd |
| L | 18 | Walter F Pitts | Rose & Crown |
| | 19 | Jessy Blazey | People St |
| | 20 | William Jacobs | Fairland |
| L | 21 | Harriett White | do |

*Non-parochial registers of baptism and burial are not the only sources for locating dissenters. This list of the members of a local Methodist society is informative in that it indicates by 'L' those who left the society, and by 'D' those who died.*

that the same ancestor or his family was buried in the parochial churchyard would not necessarily indicate reversion back to the Church of England; a more likely explanation might, according to the period, be that the chapel had not yet acquired a burial ground of its own. Some Anglican clergy who buried non-conformists in their churchyard were apt to label them in their registers as 'Anabaptists', regardless of what denomination they belonged to.

Early non-conformist congregations suffered persecution or restriction, and these experiences may have been recorded. The Quakers have a wealth of historical archives at Friends' House; the Baptists, Congregationalists and Presbyterians have their own historical societies; and the Methodists have archivists for each of their administrative areas. Descendants of non-conformist ancestors should also consult the printed works and manuscripts at Dr Williams's Library, once called the Dissenters' Library, at 14 Gordon Square, London WC1.

Ancestors' religious opinions may be revealed in their Last Wills and Testaments. These documents, due for submission to ecclesiastical courts for probate, usually started with a religious preamble commending the testator's soul to God. The manner in which this was worded is an indication of the religious opinions of somebody, but whether that somebody was the testator himself or a lawyer who drew up the will, or the scrivan (clerk) who wrote it out, may be difficult to decide, though for a document in which commendation of one's soul took priority a testator is likely to have employed the services of a co-religionist. Any reference to a hope of being among the Elect is an indication of Calvinism. Bequests made to the parish church, the 'mother church' (cathedral of the diocese) and the poor of the parish are indications of being Church of England.

In August 1558 the will of Jane Fitzhugh, widow, made her religious faith very clear:

> I bequeath my soul unto Almighty God to be presented through the meek intercession of the most glorious Virgin Mary and the holy communion of heaven. . . . To a priest to sing for my soul and my husband's soul and for all my friends' souls and all Christian souls, £10.

But, as far as the priest's intercession was concerned, Jane's request was frustrated through her survival until the following summer. By that time Catholic Queen Mary was dead, Protestant Queen Elizabeth was on the throne, and prayers for the souls of the dead were proscribed.

There have been two periods of English history during which the religious life of the whole population has been thrown into turmoil. The first was the Reformation, covering the reigns of Henry VIII, Edward VI and Mary I and into that of Elizabeth I. The process of change from Catholicism to Protestantism swayed to and fro for half a century, and ordinary people had to watch their steps. *Letters and Papers of the Reign of Henry VIII* and *State Papers (Domestic)* contain decrees banning certain books as heretical or subversive, refusal to translate the Bible into English, and other efforts to keep the populace in step with the current monarch's policy. My own family was split between a Catholic head of the family and his Protestant brother, who, as a Justice of the Peace, was responsible for bringing Catholics to 'justice'. Any family history covering this period should attempt to reflect the uncertainties and fears that shook all levels of the population.

In the next century came a period, known as the Puritan Revolution, when the Church of England's Anglican establishment was under attack from within by people of ultra-Protestant views. Clashes in parochial life may appear in parish records and also in the numerous Petitions sent in to Parliament by aggrieved groups and individuals. It was in the latter that I first discovered the side my ancestor took in these troubled times. In March 1642, the opposed Anglican and Puritan parishioners of St Olave's, Southwark, held separate meetings and elected different churchwardens. The Puritans took the precaution of getting all their voters to sign their names or make their marks, and William Fitzhugh was one of their signatories. Being therefore one of the Puritans, he probably had not altogether disapproved the violence perpetrated by them some months before in the parish church. This was described in another Petition to Parliament by the frightened Anglican curate, the Revd Oliver Whitby:

> On Sunday last, being the 6 of June [1641], in the administration of the Holy Communion, there happened a great uproar in the said church by some who are disobedient to the laws of the state and Church of England. . . . Those disturbers of God's peace and the King's, after 500 had received the sacrament kneeling, would force your petitioner to give it to them sitting, contrary to law . . . and thereupon made a great shout in the church, put on their hats, some crying: 'Lay hands on him! Kick him out of the church! Pull him by the ears! Baal's priest, bald-pate, carry home your consecrated bread and sop your pottage!' Others thronged about him, laid hands on him, reviled him and laboured to hinder those who were willing to kneel, insomuch that God's holy ordinances were much dishonoured and many good Christians affrighted

| Name | Reg. No. | Year | Date | Age (yrs) | Age (mths) | Occupation |
|---|---|---|---|---|---|---|
| William Lock | 236 | .. | .. | 6 | 0 | Dairyman |
| Emma Lock | 237 | | June | 4 | 0 | " |
| Charlotte White | 238 | " | " | 4 | . | Woodman |
| Matilda Bellisc | 239 | .. | .. | 3 | 6 | Inn Keeper |
| Mary Clark Stansford | 240 | .. | " | 4 | | Labourer |
| Cecily L. Cockerain | 241 | " | July | 6 | 5 | Schoolmaster |
| Lila May Cockerain | 242 | . | / | 3 | 2 | " |
| Sarah Cousins | 243 | .. | .. | 5 | 1 | Labourer |
| John Grinter | 244 | .. | Sep | 8 | 4 | Sea Captain |
| Elizabeth Davies | 245 | .. | Sepr | 5 | 7 | |
| Mary Hounsel | 246 | . | /. | 4 | 8 | Father dead |
| Robert Travis | 247 | 1866 | Jay | 4 | | Labourer |
| Ellen Biles | 248 | " | /. | 10 | 4 | " |
| Harriet Brown | 249 | " | Jany | 3 | 6 | |
| Joseph Lock | 250 | 1865 Augt | | 12 | 0 | Dairyman |
| Ellen Roper | 251 | " | /. | 4 | | Labourer |
| Charles Watts | 252 | 1866 Jany | | 8 | | " |
| Edward Herring | 253 | " | March | 8 | 10 | " |
| George Herring | 254 | " | " | 6 | 6 | " |

*School registers such as this give not only the child's name, but (from left to right) its registration number, date of admission, age at that time, parents' occupations, previous education, home and further details.*

from the Holy Communion that day. . . . They threaten . . . if he will not give them the sacrament next Sunday as they please, they will drag him by the heels about the church.

Stirring times. These petitions to Parliament are now to be found at the House of Lords Record Office. Once the Civil War began, religious observances in parliamentary areas were successively overturned. The *Book of Common Prayer* was done away with and a *Directory for the Public Worship of God* substituted; Sunday sports and the celebration of Christmas were forbidden. These were all changes in the lives of ordinary people, our ancestors, and therefore materials for our family history. For the innovations of this period, not only in religious matters, the *Acts and Ordinances of the Interregnum*, compiled by C.H. Firth and R.S. Rait, is essential browsing.

## Education

This aspect of an ancestor's career will largely depend upon his parents' station in life. The attendance registers of the local National School (Church of England) or British School (non-conformist) may survive either in local or county record office keeping. Alternatively, or subsequently, the boy may have been sent to the nearest grammar school. If his parents were sufficiently well off to send him to a private school followed by a public school, these may have been in any part of the country, not necessarily near home. Most public and many grammar school registers are in print. These and also the university registers are conveniently kept together in the library of the Society of Genealogists, where even non-members may search on payment of a day's, or part-of-a-day's, search fee. Some school histories have been written and may contain interesting facts about periods when our ancestors were pupils.

## Marriage

In past centuries a marriage could be initiated in several ways, either arranged by the parties' parents or permitted by their approval, or just proposed by the suitor and accepted by his lady-love. Between members of the aristocracy, among whom considerations of property and rank were usually taken into account, a marriage might be arranged. Among the gentry and middle classes, a suitor was expected to ask permission of the young woman's father to pay her his addresses or, at least, having already paid them, to ask for his permission for the marriage. If the suitor failed to come up to papa's expectations, he had to look elsewhere and the daughter of the house to wait for another admirer. Only working-class couples seem always to have had the freedom to 'keep company' before marriage. However, among most people, a strong personal preference would play its part, so this period of ancestral life can be treated as a 'love story'. Too often, though, a wooing and its successful outcome are covered by the family historian in some such words as:

> 'And on 3rd June 1846, John married Harriet, daughter of George
> Smith, apothecary, of the parish of Little Slowcombe'

— as though she had suddenly descended upon him in wedding dress when nothing was further from his thoughts. That is no way to write a love story. Marriage was the climax of a process known as 'courting'; therefore as historian you should try to find out how 'Grandpapa met Grandmama'. You will not manage to pin it down to 'the second minuet', but you may well be able to show how they would have, or could have, come to know each other. If the marriage entry in the parish register describes them as 'both of this parish', you have no difficulty; they were near neighbours, attending the same church and other functions of the ecclesiastical parish; so, with a little skill, you should be able to bring in a mention of the young woman, or at least her family, before the reader has any notion of what lies in store for the couple. You could perhaps do this when describing their home village. Her father may have been the parson or a member of the parish vestry, or the innkeeper or blacksmith, or some other person whose activities would warrant an easy mention. Or he may have been of the same occupation as the ancestor, or an allied one. In my professional searches I came across a bridegroom who described himself as 'Sergeant of the Militia', and I found that his father-in-law was a 'Military Cap-maker' in the nearest town. As historian, you would not, on the strength of that, be justified in saying that when the sergeant went to buy a new cap, there, behind the counter, stood the cap-maker's lovely daughter; but, without committing yourself to any such precision, you can set your readers' imagination working. Each one will fill in the details to his or her own satisfaction.

If the parish register shows not only that they were both of the same parish, but that they had both been baptised there, then they grew up in proximity, joined in the same church festivals, danced round the same maypole and perhaps, depending on the period, attended the same village school. If they married young, it was 'a boy and girl affair'.

More often, the bride and bridegroom will have lived in different parishes, so how did they get to know each other in the days before cars, buses or even bicycles? There were two features in rural life that regularly

*A country fair, portrayed by Thomas Rowlandson (1756-1827), shows a swain purchasing a bunch of ribbons, and the cause of his staying 'so long at the fair'.*

brought inhabitants together over a fairly wide area, the weekly or bi-weekly market at the market town, and the annual or bi-annual fair at the same place. A country village rarely had more than one tiny shop, if that; so for goods that the people could not make themselves they set out regularly for the market. On that day the town's shops were supplemented by the stalls of neighbouring farmers and traders; and they themselves might have produce to sell. With everybody congregating there, it was also a social occasion. Markets and fairs as the means of bringing young people together formed a subject for folk song, though the old versifiers tended to sing of the fair rather than the market, presumably because of the rhyme difficulty. The problem of what to do with the car had yet to arise.

> As I was going to Strawberry Fair,
> I met a maiden carrying her ware.
> Her eyes were blue, and golden her hair
> As she went on to Strawberry Fair.

And:

> Oh dear, what can the matter be!
> Johnnie's so long at the fair.
> He promised he'd buy me a bunch of blue ribbons
> To tie up my bonnie brown hair.

Beneath that bonnie brown hair lurked the suspicion that some blonde was chatting Johnnie up.

It is worth studying the map and consulting the *Victoria History* of your county, and *Lewis's Topographical Dictionary of England and Wales*, to gauge whether the parties would have shared the same market town. Once a young man was attracted, he would, in those days, have thought nothing of walking many miles to keep a tryst.

If your ancestors were what were known in some circles as 'carriage folk' they would have been able to take in a wider geographical range of acquaintance. In the local papers of the nineteenth century, the accounts of charity, county and hunt balls and other social functions included the names of those present. You may well find mentions of a young man and woman, later to become Mr and Mrs, at the same event.

From 1731, weddings reported in *The Gentleman's Magazine* might even, impertinently, mention that entirely private matter, the marriage settlement, as it did in 1769:

> Thos. Fitzhugh, Esq. to Miss Lloyd with £10,000

The dowry was a big one, which is probably why the magazine mentioned it. Miss Lloyd was a catch.

Local newspaper accounts of weddings in the nineteenth century were not as numerous as they are today, being confined to those that could, by some stretch of imagination, be described as 'fashionable', meaning those of the county gentry. These, however, were reported at considerable length, including the name or names of the officiating clergy, descriptions of the bride's, bridesmaids' and even bride's mother's dresses, together with the hymns chosen, and extracts from the parson's address, ending with a long and useful list of those relations and friends of both families who were present or had been invited.

With success in a proposal of marriage dependant on acceptance from both the young man's intended and her father, courtship was a process calling for circumspection. Matters could not be rushed. In his youth, my father (before meeting my mother) was attracted to a Miss Mabel Sugden. His diary for 1900 contains the following entry:

> *Thursday, 12th July* ... Dined with the Sugdens and bicycled

afterwards by moonlight. Had a long talk with Emmie. She says that I ought to let Mabel know everything, anyhow before I go. She also said that Mabel suspected something. Mabel told me I could call her Mabel. Hurrah!

But, being at that time a mere agricultural student, my father probably discerned no approving glint in Mr Sugden's eye. At any rate, he sailed away to the Argentine without telling Mabel 'anything'.

Until the Married Women's Property Act of 1882, a woman became at marriage a penniless creature. Her situation was spelt out in a document signed by an ancester and ancestress of mine who got married in Constantinople in 1754. To bring their marital property affairs into line with English practice, the following Marriage Agreement (*SP.105//183*) was drawn up between them:

I, Valentine Fitzhugh, in consideration of Elizabeth Palmentier's concessions, oblige and bind myself at my decease that my executors, heirs or assigns shall pay to my said wife Elizabeth Palmentier one third part of my estate, whether it be in money, lands, houses, credits, jewels etc, which, at her decease, shall be disposed of as I, Valentine Fitzhugh, shall direct by will. In consideration whereof, I, Elizabeth Palmentier, do absolutely invest the said Valentine Fitzhugh with full power and authority to seize, claim and take in his possession all moneys, jewels, credits, lands, houses, tenements and furniture or whatever I am at present possessed of or may be hereafter entitled to, and that all and every part of these effects shall be entirely at the said Valentine Fitzhugh's disposal; further declaring by these presents that I do now absolutely dispossess myself of all my effects whatsoever.

Which seems to cover everything.

That particular marriage eventually became the subject of a tradition passed down in the family by word of mouth. Such tales are told and retold in many families, and nowadays they are treated seriously by historians. They fall under two headings, *Oral History* and *Oral Tradition*. The former consists of the early personal experiences of old people related by word of mouth at first hand. Oral tradition differs in having been already passed down to the teller through one or more generations. Much oral history may of course include older traditional tales heard in the teller's youth. For the family historian, the main difference between the two lies in the amount of reliance that can be placed upon them. Every time a story is repeated it risks alteration, as in the old, though probably

This indenture (note the deckled edge) is a marriage agreement of 1712 drawn up to protect the property rights of the bride and any children she might have.

apocryphal, story of the officer at the front who sent back by a relay of messengers the urgent request, 'Send reinforcements; we are going to advance', which arrived at base as 'Send three and fourpence; we're going to a dance'. In traditional tales, tricks of memory, all too likely to occur even in first-hand recollections, can be compounded by historical misunderstandings and wishful interpretation. The oral tradition passed down about the above marriage, was that 'Valentine married a beautiful Circassian'; and the romantic bride was held to be the genetic source of the dark good looks of certain contemporaries of mine. Actually Miss Elizabeth Palmentier of Constantinople was a French Huguenot. Word-of-mouth communication across the centuries needs to be taken with a pinch of salt. Oral tradition usually consists of a core of truth in a coating of fiction, and the fiction improves the story.

Orally traditional in many families is a ghost story, which the family historian may well feel worth re-telling. We have one in our family, about the phantom coach that drove up to the front door to call for Great-Aunt Lizzie's soul. However, I will not detain you with that.

## *Private correspondence*

A few old letters are often to be found treasured by some member of the family, constituting all that can be described as family papers. Recently several family history journals have been publishing correspondence from early emigrants to their relations at home, containing fascinating details of the primitive conditions with which they were having to cope. Unfortunately, letters of a more routine nature tend to follow the easy path down to the waste-paper basket. Sometimes, however, an ancestor may have had occasion to correspond with some person who was, or later became, of sufficient distinction to have his papers preserved; and so family letters and autographs may now be hobnobbing with those of the great in some record repository. Among the vast number of *Additional MS* in the British Library MSS Library, at the British Museum, I found several letters written by Valentine Fitzhugh at Constantinople to James Porter, formerly British Ambassador there and later knighted. These supplied not only valuable additions to my knowledge of Valentine's career, but also gave me an insight into his character. In one of them he wrote:

Dear Sir,
... The 20th past [October 1762], two-thirds of Pera [the Christian residential suburb of Constantinople] was unfortunately burnt down, my house and furniture amongst the rest. My clerk had only time to save the counting house. I shall be a loser by this accident

at least D.5000,- -. For my part I always endeavour to avoid misfortunes, but when they happen they affect me very little, 'The Almighty giveth, he taketh away, Blessed be his name for ever'. It began at St Antonio's [convent] and burnt to the butchery, in all about 60 houses, and very little furniture saved. ...

This affair has so much disgusted both Mrs Fitzhugh and myself that we have taken the resolution to leave this country, for we see nothing but misery and destruction before us, for which purpose we have fixed upon Neufchatel, where there is good society, great liberty, and very cheap living, three points very essential. England would be very disagreeable to Mrs Fitzhugh as she does not talk the language. Besides, my fortune is not sufficient to live as I should choose. There I can live very genteelly, and I hope very happily.

The somewhat priggish claim that his mind was impervious to the slings and arrows of outrageous fortune followed only a few lines later by its complete contradiction is rather endearing. The full correspondence showed me that, but for a change of destination on Valentine's part, I might well now be a Swiss national.

I have recently been told of the existence of some more letters from a member of my family to a historical celebrity, in this case from my great-great-aunt Emily to Lady Byron, the poet's wife. When, on hearing this, I said that I must arrange to see them, my informant said, 'Oh, there is nothing in them of any interest whatever.' Never pay the slightest attention to such a comment. No one but you, the family historian, can tell what evidence you will find useful. It may well be that the most important items in those letters are Emily's address and the dates, revealing where she was at certain times. In this particular case, I do expect to get more than that, because at present I know of no reason at all why Emily should be writing to Lady Byron; so, even if her letters are deadly dull, they are bound to reveal a subject of correspondence hitherto unsuspected; and what may be merely implied in them may lead me on to some activity of Emily's that I should know about.

Information about collections of correspondence in private hands can be obtained, in major reference libraries, from the volumes of *Reports of the Historical Manuscripts Commission*, and also by consulting the *National Register of Archives*, but for collections catalogued by the latter you will need to have some previous idea as to what you are looking for. The Commission and National Register are both at Quality House, Quality Court, Chancery Lane, London WC2.

*The attitude struck by the men in the photograph above indicates that this was a set piece partly to show the photographer's skill. Such a picture turning up in a family album will almost certainly include an ancestor; but which one of them is he? and who are his friends?*

## Leisure activities

During the nineteenth century, sporting and other spare-time activities were plentifully reported in local newspapers. As evidence, newspaper reports are not entirely trustworthy. However, precautions can be taken. For many areas of the country, more than one local newspaper survives; so some cross checking is possible. In a case of doubt, a further precaution is to include the incident in your history by quotation from the paper. This absolves you from inaccuracy and enables you to exploit the literary style of the report, which usually has its own period charm. The following extracts from the *Sussex Advertiser* are examples of ancestral leisure activities regularly reported in nineteenth-century local papers, and therefore worth their search time.

### Cricket

East Hoathly and Neighbourhood v Lewes Priory. This match was played on Saturday last [27th June 1857] in the Priory Ground, when the outward party brought . . . a powerful eleven, the names of Picknell, Carpenter and Marchant being somewhat formidable to their adversaries. The game, however, proceeded, and for a second-rate match, any lover of this scientific game must have been satisfied. . . . On the part of the Priory Club the batting of FitzHugh, Tamplin, E. Monk and E. Beard was very creditable. . . . The dinner was in Mr Eager's usual good style . . .

*Archery*

South Saxon Archers. This society held its grand and final meeting on Wednesday [30th August 1848] in Coneyborough Park. The day was delightfully fine, and the assemblage . . . presented an imposing appearance. A commodious tent was erected, where refreshments were supplied; and in the evening the junior part of the company enjoyed themselves by dancing quadrilles. There were no less than 150 ladies and gentlemen present, who commenced shooting shortly after 12 o'clock. At half past three the company partook of an excellent repast, provided by Mr Jones of the Star Hotel. The archery was recommenced about half past four, when a first rate display of skill was afforded by the company, both by the ladies and gentlemen. The following is the result of the shooting:

Best of numbers (Gentlemen) — Mr Flood, Mr Willis, Mr Slater, Mr FitzHugh jun.

Best of numbers (Ladies) — Miss Slater, Miss F. Bonham, Miss P. Partington, Miss FitzHugh.

. . . Among the company present, we noticed the following: . . . Mrs, Miss and Mr W. FitzHugh.

In the mid nineteenth century, the booming interest in archaeology was the social phenomenon that family history presents today. The Sussex Archaeological Society's descent upon Arundel on 13th August 1857 went off as follows.

*Archaeology*

. . . The study of archaeology is growing daily more and more popular. . . . the train leaving Hastings at 9 a.m. [on 13th August 1857] and reaching Lewes at 9.15 brought a tolerable sprinkle of Archaeologists intent to avail themselves of the special train from Brighton which it was appointed to meet; but the numbers joining at Lewes were so much larger than were provided for that two extra carriages had to be put on. Brighton was reached in due course, and the carriages from Lewes were fastened on to the end of the special train, nearly the whole of the accommodation of the latter having been required for the wants of the party from Brighton and the down main line. The appearance of the train thus combined was one of a decidedly excursion character, both as regarded its magnitude and the gay appearance of the passengers who occupied it.

An unusual scene of animation [polite term for a rumpus?] presented itself at Arundel Station on the arrival of the train. Road conveyances for the transit of several hundred persons are not to be improvised, like Cinderella's coach, at a moment's notice. ... The means however were found, sufficiently ample even for the extended space required in these days by the fashionable toilets of the ladies. ... Among those present ... Mr and the Misses FitzHugh

A popular annual event was the local Horticultural Show, always attended by the FitzHughs. The three classes under which the entrants could compete with their flowers, fruit and vegetables reflected the sharply defined social class structure of the time, as did also the manner of reporting the function. At Chailey, Sussex, on 30th August 1850:

The show was held in a meadow adjoining the King's Head, where a couple of commodious booths had been erected having an internal communication, forming as it were two rooms en suite. ... The first booth was appropriated to the productions exhibited by Gentlemen's Gardeners. ... Passing from the first to the second booth, the visitor found himself among the contributions from the Amateurs. ... But however excellent the display in other classes, we confess that to our view the main interest of the exhibition was centred in the Cottagers' contributions, which were really alike creditable to their skill and industry. ... They tell of care and attention in moments snatched from long days of toil; they tell of hours spent in the quiet enjoyment of home and its endearments; hours perhaps once devoted to the vitiated but too successful attractions of the beer-shop.

And in the winter evenings there were the balls, such as the following on 12th January 1849:

The Annual Southdown [Hunt] Ball. This ball took place at the

MR. BLACK MAKING UP HIS MIND NOT TO ASCEND THE TOR.

*Nineteenth-century news-paper reports of events such as the British Archaeological Association's visit to Glastonbury and Wells ('Illustrated News' 1856) sometimes include anecdotal material of named members.*

MISS LEE OF BEAMINSTER.

We next walked up the Shepton Mallet Road towards the "Barn," Mr. Black scudding along (with his gray cloth cap and blue bag, looking like an unsuccessful lawyer who has lost his hat) in company with a thin-legged antiquary, who is only to be compared to the afternoon shadow of Mr. Davis (just arrived from Bath, having up to this moment disappointed the company, because, as he candidly observed, he "felt lazy").

"The Barn" was the storehouse of the Glastonbury abbots; they were paid in kind, and it was here that their tithes were received. It is a large square dark building, with a fine roof of the fifteenth century, and curious windows, supposed by Mr. Davis to be used for purposes of fortification. The outside of the building is ornamented with emblems of the four Evangelists.

"Do you know," said Mr. Black, as we returned from the Barn to the Refectory, or Chapel of St. Joseph of Arimathea, "why I am gathering these wild flowers? It is my way of writing to my family. When I am out, I have no time to spare to write a long letter. See! here I have gathered pimpernel and shepherd's weather-glass. I shall send them in an envelope, and that will be as good as all the letters in the world."

The Chapel of St. Joseph, with its unique Norman turret, was a subject of great admiration, Mr. Planché being very anxious that everybody should come along! he'd show them the costume. "Why, sir, there's a real *manche* sleeve on the moulding of the south door."

The whole of the exterior ornamentation was proclaimed marvellous in its luxuriance, from the "zig-zag" round the windows to the unfinished mouldings of the doors; while the crypt and well, half-hidden among the ivy and ruins, tempted some few adventurous spirits down the crazy steps, but induced none to test the sacredness of its powers by imbibing a cupful of its nauseous waters.

The Kitchen was the next object of our attention. It is principally peculiar for the capital system of ventilation which it possesses, and which is curiously enough identical with what is termed "Dyte's patent for the prevention of smoky chimneys." At each angle is a place for cooking, but the antiquaries were puzzled to accommodate the appetites of the Friars of Glastonbury to the almost utter absence of soot in the chimneys. Let us hope they were not starved.

We are glad that we have not forgotten to engrave a sketch of "Mr. Black making up his mind not to ascend the Tor," for it was a subject worthy of being remembered. *He* did not care about the Roman encampment, although Mr. Vere Irving did, and his mind was so bent upon taking rubbings from the brasses at Wells, that not all the Romans nor Irvings that ever lived could induce him to waste time in climbing such a horribly perpendicular mound. So the Tor, looming upon us wherever we went, high, solemn, and mysterious, was not visited after all, except by Mr. Vere Irving himself.

Away we drove to Wells—looking out to Brent Knoll, and seeing the cathedral towering up; while to the left, the broad expanse of fields ripen-

Corn Exchange Rooms on Friday evening and was fashionably and most numerously attended. ... The room was fitted up with much taste, wreaths and festoons of evergreens being suspended from the sides and ceiling, interspersed with flags and banners. ... We believe the credit due for this pleasing addition to the appearance of the room is due to Mr Jones of the Star Hotel. ... At an early hour the guests began to arrive, and before nine o'clock the dancing had commenced. Kirchner's band was in attendance, and their exertions gave entire satisfaction. ... A separate apartment was appropriated to the Card Room, where those not under the inspiration of Terpsichore might enjoy themselves in other fashion. Dancing was kept up with infinite spirit till a late hour in the morning — indeed some idea may be formed of the gaiety which prevailed, when we state that a little before four o'clock no less than twenty couples stood up to a country dance, in which old and young alike joined. ... All classes seemed to enjoy themselves thoroughly, and while the greatest ease prevailed, there was no one circumstance which could offend the most fastidious. The entire arrangements were extremely good and reflected much credit on Mr Jones. ... Amongst the company present we observed the following: [a long list, including, in a party] Miss FitzHugh.

In addition to covering these regularly recurring events, the same newspaper occasionally contained reports of untoward incidents in which members of the family were mentioned.

On Wednesday last [3 October 1860], as Mr Botting, the respected and well-known breeder of Sussex stock, was showing a bull to the Rev. Mr FitzHugh of Streat, the halter, a new one, slightly yielded to the animal's pressure and, getting partial liberty, it struck Mr Botting with the point of its horn, which entered the upper part of the eyebrow and cut a gash in his forehead; at the same time the ferocious animal got Mr Botting against the manger. ... Mr FitzHugh called for assistance to remove the animal, which, becoming more infuriated, got Mr Botting down and commenced trampling on him. ... Assistance coming to hand, the bull was secured and Mr Botting removed from his perilous position. ... The injuries sustained are of so serious a character as to cause considerable anxiety to his family.

To search unindexed newspaper files solely on the off chance of finding some such exceptional incident would obviously not justify the time it

HYACVM, ET LVES VENEREA.

*Grauata morbo ab hocce membra mollia     Leuabit ista forpta coctio arboris .*

would take, but if the researcher finds that his family is regularly mentioned at local sporting and social events of the kind quoted above, the searches become worthwhile and any exceptional incident gets harvested along with the rest.

## Sickness and death

These two often quite separate events in an ancestor's life have to be dealt with together here because there is little information obtainable except in connection with terminal illness.

Ever since 1st July 1837, everyone has had his last illness or injury recorded on his death certificate, together with the length of time he was attended for it by his doctor. My grandfather's certificate showed his cause of death in 1886 as:

Apoplexy, 5 days. Certified by J.B. Curgenven, M.R.C.S.

What used to be called 'an apoplectic fit' is now known as a stroke, so the first attack will have come as a sudden shock. Thanks to my practice of transcribing the names of everyone in an ancestor's street, I recognised the name of the certifier. Mr J. Brendon Curgenven, surgeon, lived almost opposite my grandfather in Craven Hill Gardens, Bayswater; so I can

## The Diseases and Casualties this Week.

| | | | |
|---|---|---|---|
| Abortive | 6 | Kingsevil | 10 |
| Aged | 54 | Lethargy | 1 |
| Apoplexie | 1 | Murthered at Stepney | 1 |
| Bedridden | 1 | Palsie | 2 |
| Cancer | 2 | Plague | 3880 |
| Childbed | 23 | Plurisie | 1 |
| Chrisomes | 15 | Quinsie | 6 |
| Collick | 1 | Rickets | 23 |
| Consumption | 174 | Rising of the Lights | 19 |
| Convulsion | 88 | Rupture | 2 |
| Dropsie | 40 | Sciatica | 1 |
| Drownd two, one at St.Kath. Tower, and one at Lambeth | 2 | Scowring | 13 |
| | | Scurvy | 1 |
| Feaver | 353 | Sore legge | 1 |
| Fistula | 1 | Spotted Feaver and Purples | 190 |
| Flox and Small-pox | 10 | Starved at Nurse | 1 |
| Flux | 2 | Stilborn | 8 |
| Found dead in the Street at St.Bartholomew the Less | 1 | Stone | 2 |
| | | Stopping of the stomach | 16 |
| Frighted | 1 | Strangury | 1 |
| Gangrene | 1 | Suddenly | 1 |
| Gowt | 1 | Surfeit | 87 |
| Grief | 1 | Teeth | 113 |
| Griping in the Guts | 74 | Thrush | 3 |
| Jaundies | 3 | Tissick | 6 |
| Imposthume | 18 | Ulcer | 2 |
| Infants | 21 | Vomiting | 7 |
| Killed by a fall down stairs at St. Thomas Apostle | 1 | Winde | 8 |
| | | Wormes | 18 |

Christned { Males — 83 Females — 83 In all — 166 }
Buried { Males — 2656 Females — 2663 In all — 5319 } Plague — 3880

Increased in the Burials this Week — 1289
Parishes clear of the Plague — 34   Parishes Infected — 96

The Assize of Bread set forth by Order of the Lord Maior and Court of Aldermen,
A penny Wheaten Loaf to contain Nine Ounces and a half, and three
half-penny White Loaves the like weight.

LEFT *An early seventeenth-century sufferer from venereal disease, and the home-concocted cure being prepared for him. The scene in the frame by the bed, and the view of the kitchen, give extra information about life and times.* RIGHT *A mortality bill showing causes of death from the plague and other diseases and accidents during one week in 1665.*

envisage a member of the family, or a servant, scurrying across the road for his urgent assistance.

In families with a high infant or child mortality, as was still common in the nineteenth century, the doctor signing the death certificates will have been an all-too-frequent visitor in the home. In order to find out whither and how far some member of the family had to hurry, often on foot, to fetch him, the best source of information for his address is of course the current local directory.

Some late eighteenth-century burial register books contain a column for Cause of Death and so make it possible, even earlier than the General Register, for the historian to prepare the reader's mind for the worst. Death from illness is an event which, like birth and marriage, the historian should not spring upon his readers. From the purely narrative point of view, he could be wasting good story material.

Illness was liable to turn the sufferer's mind towards his Will, either because it was not yet made or because changes were needed. In putting this matter in order, the testator would often mention his state of bodily health, good or bad, as well as his more important claim to be of sound mind and memory. On 3rd February 1632, when Henry Fitzhugh of Bedford made his will, he was 'weak in body', and he died three weeks later. On the following 9th January his brother William too was feeling 'somewhat sickly disposed in body', but he lingered on for nearly three months. On 12th February 1679, another William Fitzhugh was 'aged and weak in body'; but, at 79, he was probably only feeling his age, because he lived until the end of the following December.

Though discoveries of non-terminal illness are rare, in the 1720s the chronic malady suffered by Captain William Fitzhugh was mentioned several times in the journals of East Indiamen, and also in *East India House Correspondence*, as for instance when his ship, the *Derby*, was about to set out from England for Calcutta in 1726. The Secretary of the Company had to write to her Chief Mate:

> The Directors are informed that Captain Fitzhugh is so grievously affected with the gout that he is utterly unable to be removed from his bed in order to be got aboard the ship; and if he should so continue, it will be impossible for him to proceed the voyage. Wherefore the Directors order me to acquaint you that if the Captain's illness should continue so that he can't come aboard, you do then weigh anchor and proceed along with the *Essex* whenever the wind presents for moving and sailing.

However, just in time the Captain recovered sufficiently to catch up with the ship at Deal and be hauled aboard.

There are other sources of sickness and death. In 1731, ship's purser Thomas Fitzhugh's final illness, 'flux and fever', was recorded by his captain in the ship's journal; and in 1793 *The Gentleman's Magazine* mentioned that Nancy Purling, née Fitzhugh, had died 'after a short illness'.

At all periods since parish registers were introduced, exceptional causes of death, especially violent ones, moved parish incumbents to mention them in their registers. Some of these cases would become the subject of a coroner's inquest. When an interval has occurred between death and the issue of a certificate, it is likely to have been because an inquest was held, and in such cases the coroner will be entered as the 'informant'. The official coroners' inquest records are not available until after seventy-five years, but reports of the proceedings appear in the local press, and provide the family historian with sad but interesting stories. In cases of suicide it is worth remembering that until recent times, killing oneself while of sound mind was both a crime in the eyes of the law and a sin in the eyes of the Church, which was why any available evidence of mental derangement would be brought in evidence by the sorrowing relatives.

In 1609 and again in 1754 court proceedings over the will of deceased members of my family provided me with information not only about the state of their health during their last days, but also about the expectations entertained by their children. These too can be drawn upon to enable the historian to write a fuller and more interesting account of an ancestor's death than a bare mention of his burial.

A will can leave clues to the late-lamented's feelings towards his family and to the sort of person he was. When Thomas Fitzhugh, widower (1728-1800), made his will in 1799 he left bequests not only to all his children and grandchildren, but also to his brothers and sisters, their consorts and their children and grandchildren, and his brother-in-law and his wife, and also snuff-boxes, watches and mourning rings to a number of friends, conveying a strong impression of an extroverted, friendly, warm-hearted, likeable old boy.

On the other hand, my ancestress Mary Fitzhugh (1607-*c*.1650) was evidently not in her father's good book when he made his will in 1638. He left his eldest daughter land, and several younger daughters sums of £200 and £100 each, but went on to make other bequests without mentioning Mary. Then, right at the end of his will, he left her £10. Even this was probably only the legal precaution commonly resorted to by testators when cutting children out of their wills. Inserting a derisory legacy prevented them from making a claim on the estate on the grounds that the impaired condition of the testator's memory had caused him to forget them. Mary's marriage seems a likely cause of her father's disapproval, probably on religious grounds, because her Fitzhugh husband was a Puritan.

## Funerals

Death may not be your end of an ancestor's story. He had still to be borne to the churchyard. The legal requirements for all bodies to be buried wrapped in nothing but woollen may be worth mentioning as a novelty at the first family interment after the Act of 1666; but a death in the family at any date may provide something of individual interest in the funeral, or at least in how the deceased wished it to be conducted. In 1740 my ancestress Mary Fitzhugh laid down in her Will that she was to be interred:

> without any funeral pomp or pall-bearers; and it is my express will, order and request that the house in which I now live, or wherein I shall or may happen to die, be not hung with any sort of mourning of any kind.

Burial registers occasionally contain entries showing that the heart and sometimes bowels of the deceased were buried separately from the body. Instructions for this Partial Burial were given by my ancestor Valentine

Fitzhugh in 1793 in a letter (one of our few family papers) that his wife was to open at his death:

> It is my particular desire to be buried where I may die in the plainest and least expensive manner possible, for I know nothing more absurd than to throw away money idly in transporting the dead to distant places. [And] that twenty-four hours after my death I may be opened, my heart taken out and divided into two equal parts, each put into a silver box, one of which to be laid on my most honoured and most dearly beloved Mother's coffin; the other, whenever my dearest Babet may die, to be placed near her heart and buried with her; and this I intend as the last and dearest mark I can leave them of the most sincere and affectionate love I bear them.

Affecting indeed, but as far as expense goes this request by Valentine seems as contradictory as his professed and actual reactions to the burning-down of his house in Constantinople, quoted above. His granddaughter Emily, Fanny Kemble's friend, would have felt little sympathy with such a romantic gesture. In 1856 she stipulated in her Will:

> I particularly request that my funeral may be conducted in the simplest manner; that I may be interred in the nearest cemetery or village church yard; a walking funeral, to be borne by poor men to my grave; no crepe, scarves and drapery and other absurd customs of an undertaker.

And at Robert Fitzhugh's funeral in February 1609, sorrow was not the only emotion in the mourners' minds. As one witness in a Star Chamber suit gave evidence:

> Upon the day of the burial of the said Robert Fitzhugh there was days appointed to search as well for more writings as also for money and plate.

And that was the beginning of a legal battle over his estate that lasted more than a decade — and provided me with a whole chapter for my history.

The documentary sources mentioned in this chapter apply to an ancestor in his capacity of private person, but they do begin to round out his brief entry on the family tree into a once-living member of the family. There are, of course, a number of other aspects of his life and character that can be discovered, and these we will examine in turn.

# 9   The ancestor as breadwinner

In this chapter we follow the male members of the family in their occupations. First we need to find out what each man's occupation was. Throughout the nineteenth century this is not difficult. Census Returns back to 1841, birth, marriage and death certificates to 1837, and baptismal registers back to 1813 routinely reveal such information. For self-employed people it can be supplemented by trade directories well back into the eighteenth century. In still earlier times, there are occasional mentions of a person's occupation in parish register entries, particularly when more than one family of the same name lived in the locality.

Other sources of information as to a man's occupation are the probate records. In making a will, the testator began by identifying himself with a statement of his name, parish, and either occupation or status. This last will be either esquire, gentleman, yeoman, citizen or husbandman — descriptions that can be deceptive. When a man retired from gainful employment, he would often describe himself as 'gentleman', although while still working he would not have been considered such. The term 'husbandman' usually indicates the status of a smallholder who also worked for an employer, but it can also designate the occupation of quite a prosperous cultivator of the soil, paying more tax than many yeomen or gentlemen. 'Esquire' can also be confusing. Strictly used it indicated the holder of a commission under the Crown, but these were of many kinds. In the army, all officers were esquires; but in the navy only captains, since other officers received their commissions from their commander. Among the many bearers of the designation in civilian life was the public hangman. In London, a middle-class testator might describe himself as 'Citizen and Draper'. This would mean that he was a freeman of the City and of the Drapers Company. It would not mean, except by coincidence, that he was a draper himself.

ABOVE *A late nineteenth-century photograph of a milkman and his cart. The signboard behind gives information about rents of the day.* RIGHT *Inventories often list tools of the deceased's trade, as does this one of Francis Laugher, linen weaver, who died in 1715. In his workshop were two looms, a valuable quantity of flax, yarn and woven cloth, and miscellaneous other equipment.*

Another probate record useful for discovering a man's occupation is the inventory of a deceased person's goods and chattels, if one was made. This could list the tools of his trade and, if he was self-employed, quite large items of movable equipment.

If a person was ever involved in a law suit, even if only as a witness, his occupation or status was entered in the records of the case.

Another type of record provides us with a first step for following an ancestor's working career: namely an apprentice binding. Apprentices were of two kinds: trade apprentices bound by their parents to a master to learn a trade; and poor apprentices, children of either sex, put out by parish officials to service with local farmers or other householders, the boys to learn husbandry and the girls housewifery. The records of poor apprentices are to be sought at the county record office, in vestry minutes, the accounts of Churchwardens and Overseers of the Poor, and sometimes in Quarter Sessions records.

A TRUE and perfect Inventary of all the Goods and Chattells of ffrancis Sampere Weaver Late of Stoak Prior dec'd taken and apprais'd the thirtieth day of December 1715 by us whose names are hereunto subscribed (viz.)

| | £ — s — d |
|---|---|
| Imprimis Money in Purse and wearing Apparrell | 3 — 0 — 0 |
| Item In the Hall Seaven pewter dishes two douzen of Plates Seaven porringers | 2 — 11 — 5 |
| two Kettles one Pott | 0 — 10 — 0 |
| One warming pan a frying pan a Skimmer a pair of brass Scales a Smoothing iron and Heaters | 0 — 08 — 0 |
| One firegrate fireshovell tongs and firelink a pair of bellows one Chaffing dish two Candlesticks Six Chaires a Douzen of trenchers one Lanthorne | 0 — 09 — 6 |
| In the Buttery ffour barrells with other odd things | 0 — 08 — 0 |
| In the Bakehouse One furnace two tubbs one Steele two Peeles one Gawne one Chopping block a Chopping Knife | 1 — 06 — 0 |
| Itid. In the Chamber one pair of Bedsteads with Curtins and vallens one feather bed a bolsters two blankotts one Coverlett two Coffers four boxes four pair of Sheets | 06 — 11 — 0 |
| Itid. fflax | 19 — 17 — 0 |
| Itid. Yarne | 16 — 01 — 1 |
| Itid. three peices of flaxen Cloath | 00 — 10 — 0 |
| Itid. two Loomes | 04 — 0 — 0 |
| Eight Geer's and Slay's and other odd things in the Shopp with barr & Sear's | 02 — 13 — 0 |
| Itid. 12 pair of Slatches | 00 — 16 — 0 |
| Itid. Some Coke and Coles | 00 — 17 — 0 |
| | |
| Tot. | 67 — 12 — 2 |

Wr. Perkes
Tho. Miles
Rich. Sampere Juni.
apprs.

**His Indenture** made the _fifth_ — — Day of _June_ — in the _Second_ Year of the Reign of our Sovereign _Lord Lady Anne_ — — by the Grace of God of _England, Scotland, France,_ and _Ireland_, _Queen_ — Defender of the Faith, &c. Annoq; Dom. 1703 _Witnesseth_, That _John Austy Jun. & William Galpin_ — — — of _Dorset_ — Church-Wardens of the Parish of _Wimborne_ in the _County_ — and _Anthony Barham_ _John King, Oliver Batt & Richard Reynolds_ Overseers of the Poor of the said Parish, by and with the Consent of _Her_ — Majesties Justices of the Peace of the said _County_ — — whose Names are hereunto subscribed, have put and placed, and by these Presents do put and place _Jeffrey Harvey_ — — a poor Child of the said Parish, Apprentice to _Thomas Barnes of Wimborne Minster, Dorset, Yeoman_ — with him to dwell and serve from the Day of the Date of these Pesents, until the said Apprentice shall accomplish his full Age of _four & twenty years_. During all which Term, the said Apprentice his said Master faithfully shall serve in all lawful Businesses, according to his power, wit, and ability; and honestly, orderly and obediently, in all things demean and behave him self towards his said Master and all his during the said term. And the said _Thomas Barnes_ — for himself, his Executors and Administrators, doth Covenant and Grant to and with the said Church-Wardens and Overseers, and every of them, their and every of their Executors and Administrators, and their and every of their Successors, for the time being, by these Presents, That the said _Thomas Barnes_ — shall and will, during all the term aforesaid, find, provide and allow unto the said Apprentice, meet, competent and sufficient Meat, Drink, and Apparel, Lodging, Washing, and all other things necessary and fit for an Apprentice. And also shall and will so provide for the said Apprentice, that he be not any way a Charge to the said Parish, or Parishioners of the same; but of and from all Charge shall and will save the said Parish and Parishioners harmless and indempnified during the said term. And at the end of the said term, shall and will allow and deliver unto the said Apprentice Apparel of all sorts. In Witness whereof, the Parties abovesaid to these present Indentures interchangeably have put their Hands and Seals the Day and Year above-written.

Sealed and Delivered in the Presence of

WE whose Names are subscribed, Justices of the Peace of the County — aforesaid do consent to the putting forth of the abovesaid _Jeffrey Harvey_ Apprentice, according to the intent and meaning of the Indenture abovesaid.

_Antho: Barham_
_Oliver Batt_
_Richard Reynolds_
_John + King_

_Jeffrey Harvey, 'a poor child', is bound apprentice in 1703 by the Churchwardens and Overseers of the Poor to yeoman Thomas Barnes, 'with him to dwell and serve' until the age of 24. Two Justices of the Peace, the named six churchwardens and overseers (one marks with a cross) approve the indenture._

Later occupational evidence of boys who have been poor apprentices and become farm workers may be discoverable if the local land-owning family have deposited their old estate account books at the county record office, as many have. They contain details of work done by employees and wages paid. Domestic servants too, male and female, may be mentioned in them by name.

Trade apprenticeships were governed by the *Statute of Labourers and Apprentices* of 1563, which enacted that no person should exercise any craft or mystery in a market town unless he had first served an apprenticeship of at least seven years. At his binding to a master, the boy had to be over ten and under eighteen years of age, and could not attain his freedom until he was at least twenty-one. He had to be the son of a freeman, 'not occupying husbandry' and not a labourer; and his master must be a householder exercising an 'art, mystery or manual occupation'.

In corporate towns, special conditions were applied to merchants, drapers, goldsmiths, ironmongers, embroiderers and clothiers. They could only be masters of either their own sons or sons of a parent having an estate of inheritance or freehold of at least 40 shillings a year. A longer list of such conditions for other trades is to be found in my *Dictionary of Genealogy*.

From the year 1710 a stamp duty was levied on all trade apprentice bindings in which the indenture fee paid by the parent to the master was at least one shilling, and the register of these transactions is among the Inland Revenue records at the Public Record Office, Kew (IR.1 and Index IR.17). This shows the names of the apprentice, his father (or mother if she was widowed), and his master, with the latter's trade or livery company, and the abodes of them all. After 1760 the information often omits the parent's name. By 1767 the maximum age for an apprentice was reduced from 24 to 21. Compulsory binding to the specified trades was ended in 1814. An index of the Inland Revenue records, 1710-74, is available at the Society of Genealogists and the Guildhall Library, London. The Society also has a collection of original indentures.

Apart from the Inland Revenue records, the apprentice registers of nearly all the livery companies of the City of London from the sixteenth century onwards are now available at the Guildhall Library. Those of provincial corporate boroughs will be found at their borough or county record offices.

Apprentice bindings before 1733 will be in Latin, as in the following example from the *Merchant Taylors Company's Apprentice Bindings*:

> Willelmus Fitzhugh, filius Roberti Fitzhugh de Barford in comite Beddford, yeoman, posuit se apprentice Edvardo Peirce de London bridg pro novem annis a festo sancti Michaelis Archiangelis ultimo pter Dat undecimo die Octobris Anno domini 1613 Annoque Regni Jacobi Anglie primeri undecimo.

In English:

> William Fitzhugh, son of Robert Fitzhugh of Barford in the county of Bedford, yeoman, placed himself apprentice to Edward Peirce of London Bridge for nine years from the feast of St Michael the Archangel last. Dated the 11th day of October A.D.1613 and in the eleventh year of the reign of James the First of England.

The quarter days (Lady Day 25th March), the Nativity of St John the Baptist (Midsummer Day, 24th June), Michaelmas (29th September) and

Christmas Day were traditional dates for starting and terminating contracts of all kinds.

As already mentioned, one cannot assume that a London master's occupation was indicated by the name of his company. Edward Peirce was not a taylor but a draper — and yet there was a Drapers Company. The joint designation worded 'Citizen and Merchant Taylor' always means that the latter term — in this case Merchant Taylor — is the name of the person's livery company, freedom of which was his qualification for being a Citizen of London. Nor is it safe to assume when an apprentice gained his freedom he followed the trade of his former master. The above-mentioned William Fitzhugh became neither draper nor tailor but a hosier, a trade he may have learnt while he was a journeyman before being able to set up in business for himself. Journeyman, by the way, is a word derived from the French *journée*, and means an employee coming in to work and paid by the day. It had nothing to do with travelling.

Having found an apprentice binding in a livery company list, the record of his freedom should then be looked up. According to the company, it will look something like this, from the *Fishmongers Company Freemen's List*:

> Quinto die Decembris Anno Supradicto [1712]   Robertus Fitzhugh, filius Willelmi Fitzhugh, nuper Apprenticius Roberti Garbrand, liberi, clamans Libertatem per Servicium, admissus et Juratus est.

In English:

> 5th December in the aforesaid year [1712]   Robert Fitzhugh, son of William Fitzhugh, formerly apprentice of Robert Garbrand, freeman, claiming freedom by servitude, is admitted and sworn.

Here again, though Robert Garbrand was a freeman of the Fishmongers Company, he was in fact a linen-draper; and his apprentice followed him in that trade.

When a young man became free of a City livery company, he then applied for the freedom of the City, without which he could not set up in business there for himself; the records of these freedoms, from 1681 onwards, are available on postal application from the Clerk of the Chamberlain's Court, The Guildhall, London EC2.

In time, a freed apprentice was liable himself to become a master of apprentices; and the records of the apprentices bound to him can provide some indications of his progress in business. For example, an Inland Revenue entry of 1726 reads:

11/98. 1726. Blackhall, John, son of Offspring Blackhall, deceased; apprenticed to Robert Fitzhugh, Citizen and Fishmonger. Consideration: £157.10s.

In the middle of young Blackhall's servitude, his master took on a second apprentice, whose father had to pay an indenture fee of £210; and, only a year after that, a third lad was taken on and his father was charged £315. From these apprentice records one can deduce that the master's business was steadily increasing both in volume and reputation.

In the nineteenth century, when a young member of my family was being trained for an army career in India, I was able to find term by term reports not only on the progress of his studies, but also on his behaviour at the now defunct Royal Indian Military College, Addiscombe (IOLR, L/MIL/9/342), as under:

5th Class                                              First Term, May 1854
**Mathematics**

| Rank | Names | Subject of Study | Progress or Proficiency | Behaviour |
|------|-------|------------------|-------------------------|-----------|
| 22 | A. Fitzhugh | Geometry | Satisfactory | Very correct |

From knowing what profession or trade an ancestor entered, the next step is to find out what sort of work his occupation involved at that period of history. In 1747 there appeared a useful book called *The London Tradesman* by R. Campbell. In it the author described what was required of young men employed in any one of a large number of trades. Although he was writing with London in mind, his accounts would seem applicable to tradesmen of any town in the country. For linen-drapers (my interest at that period), his comments were:

> The Linen-Draper is a tradesman of considerable stock and a very useful member of society. By his retailing of linen cloth of all sorts he employs [indirectly, by marketing their products] a vast number of hands both in Scotland and Ireland and vends the linens of Germany, France and Holland ...
>
> His skill consists in a perfect knowledge of the linen manufacture in general, the difference between the different fabrics and the properties of the linens of all different countries. His business, as he is a mere buyer and seller of one particular commodity, is easily acquired, but his education ought to be genteel, as his stock in business entitles him to the first rank of tradesman. A youth may be bound to this trade between fourteen

and fifteen years of age . . . Unless a lad has a rational prospect of setting up for himself in any of these branches of the retail business, it is more than madness to serve an apprenticeship of seven years. The trader may find his account in taking a lad who has nothing for seven years, as he saves him the expence of a servant, but when that youth is out of his time and [has] spent the most precious part of his life in learning to weigh and measure out a . . . yard of ribbon, he is as much to seek for bread or any way of earning it as ever.

Presumably Robert Fitzhugh's apprentices, with fathers able to pay high fees, all had rational prospects of setting up for themselves.

Campbell's book is not the only source of information on occupations now altered out of recognition. Today's business companies that are the successors of the eighteenth-century's individual employers are usually members of a trade association for the protection of their common interests, and I have found that letters to the General Secretaries of such associations, enquiring about published histories of their trade or manufacture, are very productive of helpful answers. Through one such enquiry, I was interested to discover that my seventeenth-century hosier ancestor was operating just at the important turning-point in his trade brought about by the invention of framework knitting.

Other useful sources of information on early manufacturing processes are old encyclopedias. At sales, I have picked up *Blackie's Popular Encyclopaedia* of 1841, and the 8th Edition (1853) of the *Encyclopaedia Britannica*. The light they shed on Britain's manufactures and scientific

*Knight's 'Cyclopaedia of the Industry of All Nations', 1851, illustrates up-to-date technology, including 'flax heckling' in linen manufacture.*

## BOOT AND SHOE MAKERS

+ Atkin John, Sturston ln
* Beardsall John, Compton
Brandrith Luke, Butchery
Brandrith Thos. King st
Cope Joseph, Market place
Harrison Thos. Derby New rd
Hollis Robt. Dig st
Howell John, & toy warehouse
   Market place
Johnson Samuel, warehouse,
   St John's st
* Land Wm.
Potter Charles, Church st
* Smith James
Street Joseph, Church st
* Stubbs John, Clifton ln
Tarr Wm. Dig st
Tatlock Thos. Market place
Wigley John, Market place
Willis Thos. Butchery

## BRASS FOUNDERS

Davenport Wm. Market pl
Harlow B. Wyatt, St John's st
Haywood James, Market pl

## BRAZIERS AND TINNERS

Allen Joseph, Market place
Barnes Thos. Butcher's row
Howard Geo. Back lane
Howard Gervase, Dig st

## BRICKLAYERS

+ Brown Elisha (maker)
   Compton
+ Brown Thomas, Compton
+ Brown Wm. Compton

## BRICKMAKERS

(See Bricklayers,)

## BUTCHERS

Etches Mary Ann, Butchery
Froggatt George, Butchery
Frost Richd. (pork) Church st
Marples John and George,
   Butcher's row
Miers Wm. Butchery
Needham Wm. Butchery
Spencer Saml. Butcher's row
Tomlinson Wm. St John's st

## CABINET MAKERS

(See Joiners.)

## CHEMISTS & DRUGGISTS

Baker Harriet, St John's st
Genniss John, Market place
Greaves George Brailsford,
   St John's st
Whitham John, St John's st

## COACH BUILDERS

+ Hall Thos. & Son, Compton

## CONFECTIONERS

Bass John, St John's st
Porter James, Butchery

## COOPERS

Eyre George, Church st
Needham Robert, Market pl
Williams George, Market pl

## CORN FACTORS

Bass John, St John's st
* Eaton Joseph, Compton
Oakedon Edward, Church st

## CORN MILLER

* Eaton Joseph

## CURRIERS AND LEATHER CUTTERS

Boam Jonathan, King st
Hobson John, Market place
Spencer John, Market place

## EMERY AND COLOUR MANUFR.

* Handley Thomas, Compton

## FIRE & LIFE OFFICE AGENTS

Farmers and Graziers, John
   Hardstaff, St John's st
Manchester, Robert Hobson,
   Market place
Norwich Union, Thos. Barnes,
   St John's st
+ Phœnix Fire and Pelican
   Life, Ph. Dawson, Compton
Sun, Harriet Swindell, Mar-
   ket place
Yorkshire, John Hardstaff, St
   John's st

## GLASS, CHINA, AND EARTHEN-WARE DEALERS

Eadin Elizabeth, Market pla
Smith Fanny, St John's st

## GROCERS & TEA DEALERS

Marked * Tallow Chandlers

* Barnes Thos. Butcher's row
Bradley Septimus & Nephew,
   Market place
Clark John, Dig st
Coxon Thos. St John's st
Foster Thos. Market place  *
Genniss John, Market place
Hall Ralph Hudson, Mkt. pla
Hardstaff John, St John's st
Mellor Thos. St John's st
* Mountfort Thos. John, Mar-
   ket place
Tomlinson Jno. (late Heaton)
   Market place
Tomlinson John, Market pla
Walker Samuel, St John's st

## HAIR DRSSRS. & PERFUMERS

Poole Edward, Dig st
Redfern Luke, Dig st
Shipley Wm. & fishing tackle
   manufacturer, St John's st
Wilson Wm. St John's st

## HATTERS

(See also Drapers)

Barton Rt. (mfr.) Smith's yd
Hooworth Wm. St John's st

## HOP AND SEED MERCHANTS

Edensor Wm. Back lane
Foster Thos. Market place
Hall Ralph Hudson, Mkt pla
Morris James, St John's st
Tomlinson John, (late Hea-
   ton) Market place

## HOSIER

Tunnicliff John, St John's st

## IRONFOUNDER

* Bassett James, Compton

## IRONMONGERS

Allen Joseph, Market place
Barnes Thos. Butchers' row
Haywood James, Market place
Howard Gervase, Market pl

## JOINERS & CABINET MAKERS

Marked * are Builders.

* Birch Charles, Spital hill

*A page from the 'Directory of Derbyshire 1846', which shows Ashbourne's tradesmen and their whereabouts in the town, and conveys an idea of the local extent of each trade and the competition.*

knowledge in the middle period of the Industrial Revolution makes them more valuable for the family historian than any modern encyclopedia. In addition to the technical processes they describe, they express interesting views on the stage of industrial achievement of their age. In 1820 my great-great-grandfather had a share in the first steamboat to ply between Southampton and the Isle of Wight. The above-mentioned *Blackie's Encyclopaedia* provided an illustrated explanation of the engineering principles involved in constructing paddle-steamers, and also:

> The advantages of steam navigation have, as is well known, been immense and are daily increasing; but it is at the same time worthy of observation that the advantages to mankind by its application to the art of war are by no means inconsiderable; for by diminishing the chance of victory of either side of the combattants over the other by chance advantages of winds or currents, it increases the certainty of destruction and proportionally lessens the desire for battle.

Let us hope that confidence in our modern deterrent will prove better placed.

Indirect but revealing information on trades and manufactures and the crises they experienced at various periods of history is contained in the statute laws of the land. Throughout the whole history of Parliament, the Lords and Commons have found frequent need to regulate, promote or amend our country's trades, manufactures, imports, exports, shipping, etc.; and the laws they passed in so doing throw useful light on the commercial and industrial practices of their day — even on one occasion to the stuffing of feather beds. These laws have been catalogued in several series of volumes under the titles of *Statutes of the Realm, Statutes at Large* and *Acts and Ordinances of the Interregnum.* In each statute, a summary of the new practice laid down is prefaced by an account of the need for legislation; and to the family historian, both can be equally interesting. I have mentioned that in the sixteenth and early seventeenth centuries my family were maltsters. Pickering's *Statutes at Large* supplemented my knowledge of John Fitzhugh's trade by the following:

### 1548. The Bill for True Making of Malt

> Where divers and sundry persons taking upon them the art and mystery of malt making, and sundry other persons, tendering more their own private lucre, gain and profit than the wholesome victualling of the King's Majesty, the nobility of this realm and other his Grace's subjects, have now of late by their insatiable, covetous and greedy minds, accustomably and commonly made

the same malt in eight or nine days, where indeed the same cannot be well and perfectly made unless it have the time and space of twenty-one days in the making thereof ...

For remedy therof ... no such person or persons at any time after the first day of March next coming shall make any barley malt (the months of June, July and August only excepted), but that the same shall have in making thereof ... in the fat, floor, steeping and sufficient drying of the said malt three weeks at the least ...

And after a bad harvest in 1594, in my family's next generation, the Privy Council issued a Restraint Order on the sale of barley for malt making, and three years later came another Statute on the trade. All grist to the mill.

In the eighteenth century, my ancestors were engaged abroad in the service of chartered companies, so I shall deal with the records of such employment in a separate chapter on expatriates.

Among the professions, those of the armed services are by far the best provided with biographical evidence, both of foreground and background nature. Their official archives are housed at the Public Record Office, Ruskin Avenue, Kew, and are the subject of PRO free leaflets. However, most army regiments have also commissioned histories giving accounts of campaigns in which each battalion has taken part. In these, officers are often mentioned by name, and men of other ranks occasionally. Copies of these can be consulted at the National Army Museum, Royal Hospital Road, Chelsea, London SW3, for which a reader's ticket is necessary. Each regiment also has its own museum, and addresses of these are obtainable at Chelsea. The following is the chilling beginning of a fairly typical extract from *Campaigns and History of the Royal Irish Regiment*, describing a battle in the South African War in which my uncle Terrick FitzHugh was engaged as a 23-year-old lieutenant:

Long before daybreak on the 7th [July 1900], the troops began to take their places for the renewed attack; and the Royal Irish stumbled over the uneven surface of the veldt until they were halted at daybreak by Colonel Guiness, who pointed out to his officers the dim outline of a kopje just visible in the uncertain light. This hill, he said, General Clements considered the key of the position: it was to be taken at all cost. The Royal Irish had been selected to deliver the assault ...

For men in the Royal Navy and detailed descriptions of battles at sea, an excellent source is *The Naval History of Great Britain* by William James

(1847). In the Napoleonic Wars, my ancestor's brother Henry left school at the age of eleven to become a midshipman, and in the spring of 1808 was aboard the *Tartar* on his first voyage. His ship attacked several Danish vessels off the Norwegian port of Bergen, and her logbook for the 16th May reads:

> The attack lasted for an hour and a half, during which time they hulled us in 5 (I believe 6) places between wind and water and several other shot in the topside and many through the sails and rigging. Killed, as above: Captain Bettesworth, whom we all deplore, having lost in him a brave experienced commander who had attached all the officers and seamen to him by every part of his conduct; and Mr Fitzhugh, a promising fine lad, midshipman. Wounded: Thomas Calvo, who lost his right arm, and William Smith, seaman, severely, and several others slightly ...

At that time, Henry's father was a Member of Parliament on the government side, which situation, when I progress so far in my history, will give me an opportunity to make something of Foreign Secretary Canning's unavailing efforts to prevent Denmark from re-entering the war, a failure to be seen by my readers in retrospect as an approaching threat to the life of the then Winchester schoolboy.

In the next generation two members of my family took up careers in the law, and I found that local newspapers of the nineteenth century regularly provided accounts of my grandfather's appearances in Quarter Sessions, either for the prosecution or defence. The following, from the *Sussex Advertiser* of 3rd June 1851 is a typical report:

### East Sussex Adjourned Sessions

Eliza Brown, 20, and Catherine Avery, 19, were charged with stealing from the person of Trayton Hobbes at Brighton a half-crown, 11 shillings, 7 sixpences and 1 fourpenny piece. Mr FitzHugh conducted the prosecution, and Mr Creasey defended the prisoner Avery.

The prisoners are of the class called 'unfortunate girls', and it appeared that when the policeman, after the theft, went to the room which they occupied, Brown confessed to taking the money and handed it over. It was not so clear that Avery was acting in a common purpose with her. Brown was convicted and Avery was acquitted. A former conviction being proved against Brown, she was sentenced to six months' hard labour.

When a family's breadwinner died, his widow was by Common Law entitled to her dower, one third of her late husband's personal estate, and this did not need to be mentioned in his will. Sometimes the customary law of the manor in which a family lived altered that proportion to one quarter or one half. Any children were also assured of one third of personalty between them, leaving one third to be distributed as the testator wished. Real estate, however, descended by Common Law to the heir unless specifically bequeathed otherwise by will. The heir was the eldest son. If there were no sons but only daughters, they were all equal co-heirs. However, testamentary law underwent alterations from time to time.

Until the Married Women's Property Act of 1882 a woman's marriage, as already mentioned, transferred all her property to her husband, though if she had been married before, anything she had been left by her previous husband may have been legally safeguarded to her and any children of that marriage by a marriage settlement. In a will, a testator with a daughter is often seen to leave property, not to her but to her husband (his son-in-law) for life and then to her; this was not to her detriment, but to safeguard a long-term interest. Had the property been left immediately to her, it would in fact have legally gone to her husband, who would have owned it absolutely and been free to bequeath much of it elsewhere.

From 1796 to 1857, the approximate value of a deceased person's estate passing by will or letters of administration can be gleaned from the records of the Estate Duty Office, housed at the Public Record Office, Chancery Lane, London, in classes IR26 and 27. But earlier than that, some indication as to how well off the testator was can be gleaned from the will itself. Once his real estate and provision for his wife have been specified, he will usually leave sums of money to any daughters and younger sons. These bequests may be in single figures or in tens, hundreds or thousands of pounds each, and be correspondingly revealing. In any case, his will and, later, estate duty liability are the best indications one is likely to find as to an ancestor's financial position in life.

*Early photographs abound showing houses and householders, with helpful indications of status.*

# 7

# The ancestor as householder

Our ancestors' closest human context was their family: parents, wives, siblings and children; and their most intimate material background was the home they lived in. The readers of a family's story will hope to learn where, in each generation, their dwelling stood and what its local situation was; and will be delighted to be taken indoors and told what rooms there were, what furniture and what servants, if any, lived there too. In each case, the historian should be able to provide one or two of these insights at least partially, so I will run through the documents and devices I have found informative for my family. First, the buildings themselves and their whereabouts.

The home of the earliest-known Fitzhughs was the easiest of all for me to find. From the Middle Ages to the mid sixteenth century, my ancestors were lords of the manor of Beggary, which (now cosmeticised as Begwary) is situated in the parish of Eaton Socon, at that time in Bedfordshire; so the *Victoria History* of that county, largely devoted to tracing the descents of manors, describes the moated manor house as it existed at the beginning of this century. When, some years ago now, I went to have a look at it, the moat still surrounded the site on three sides, but the half-timbered farm house was almost certainly built after my family moved away.

The next ancestral home of which I found any descriptive evidence was that of Robert Fitzhugh (1573-1647) in the village of Lavendon, Buckinghamshire. At the county record office I discovered among the *Deeds Deposited* a Conveyance showing Robert's purchase, for £61, in 1629 of a property named the White House with a pightle (irregularly shaped piece of land) adjoining it; and several strips of arable land that went with it in the open fields. These it located in the customary manner, which was by mentioning the holdings they adjoined. One piece, for instance, was:

One rood of arable land (be it more or less) lying in Windmill Field on Plumtree Croft, [having] the land of Mr Parker, in the occupation of Edmund Eids, on the one side, and the land belonging to the Hospital of St John's of Bedford, in the occupation of widow Rogers, on the other side.

In the same generation, Robert's brothers, Henry and William, maltsters in Bedford, both left wills containing details of their homes. William's (Archd Beds. 1633) mentioned that his house, called the Green House, stood on the west side of the High Street and backed on to Duck Lane. His itemisation of the property included a second house recently built in his yard, the 'broad gates' that served as the entrance to both, and his herb garden, orchard, little barn, malting, furnace and brewing-vessels, and went on to mention the parlour with its court-cupboard, long table and six high joint stools.

Few country families can be without at least one son who was drawn away from his home village by the hope of better prospects in a nearby town or even a quite distant city, and especially to London; and my family was no exception. Robert of Lavendon, mentioned above, apprenticed his son William to a draper who lived in the first house on Old London Bridge from the Surrey side; and when the young man set up a hosiery business for himself I knew it was still situated on the southern portion of the bridge, because the mentions of him in the records of the St Olave's Precinct of Bridge Ward Within showed him somewhere between the Southwark bank and the drawbridge, which was situated a third of the way across the river. At that end of the bridge, the houses formed a continuous building line with those on the bank. The Bear Inn, on *terra firma* at what was called the Bridge Foot, shared a wall with the first house on the bridge. A stranger approaching London from the south might not realise he was on the bridge until he reached the Gate House with its portcullis, by which time he would be already over the second pier from the Surrey bank.

In trying to establish the exact position of William's house, I found a clue in two *Lists of Inhabitants of St Olave's Precinct of Bridge Ward Within* for the years 1635 and 1636. The likeness and the differences between the two were instructive. In the 1636 list, the first thirteen names of the previous year still appeared first, but in reversed order, and they were followed by the last seventeen, also in reverse order. The second enumerator had clearly started from the same side of the bridge as his predecessor, but from the opposite end of the precinct. His retention of the basic order of the names — apart from one or two newcomers — showed that it was the actual order of the residents; and the first and last names on both lists (one of which happened to be William Fitzhugh's) indicated which were the occupants of the end houses. The question was: which half of the list referred to the residents on the west side of the bridge, and which to those on the east?

Among the *Rental Books of the Bridge House Committee* I found the tenants of the two sides listed separately under East and West headings. They showed that William Fitzhugh lived on the west. But as he was in an end house, I wanted to know which end, the one near the drawbridge or the one at the Bridge Foot? Later on, during searches for other information, I found both William and his junior partner, Nathaniel Smith, separately described as 'of the Bridge Foot'. So his was the house adjoining the Bear Inn, the one formerly rented by his master and in which he had spent his apprentice years.

Placing a house by comparing householders' lists drawn up in different years is a technique applicable to other city streets, and conclusions are sometimes made easier by the mention of one building, such as an inn or coffee house, of which the exact situation is already known. However, when I wanted to locate another London house two generations later, I had no such lists to go on, so I exploited the differences between the boundaries of the city's parishes and those of its wards. In this connection, the Guildhall Library's booklets listing their records of ward and parish rate assessments, vestry minutes and churchwardens' accounts are invaluable.

I knew from an eighteenth-century Chancery case and also from a London trade directory of 1740 that Robert Fitzhugh, linendraper, lived in Cheapside, and from finding him in the parish registers and vestry minutes of St Peter's Westcheap, I knew that his shop was in the western half of the street. A map of the City showing parish boundaries showed it as more likely to be on the north side than the south. Then, in the City's Land Tax records I found Robert listed in Cripplegate Ward Within. This narrowed the area within which he lived to a short stretch on the north side, lying within both that ward and that parish. Next I examined the order of the names in both the Land Tax lists and the Poor Rate Assessments of the parish. The regularly recurring position of Robert's name in each, and the fact that his near, but not nearest, neighbours on one side were located in the directory as round the corner in Wood Street, enabled me to identify the site of his drapery as that now occupied by Pan-American World Airways.

Later in the century, London Land Tax records list the residents under street headings, which makes them easier to locate; but possible changes of street names and house numbers need to be borne in mind.

In the next generation, another 'Deed Deposited' (if that is the right term in this case) revealed some details of my ancestor's rented house in Southampton. But first, a tale that hangs thereby.

Towards the end of the 1930s my father suggested I might learn more about our early nineteenth-century ancestors if I got in touch with a long-established firm of solicitors in Southampton called Page & Moody, who had looked after our family's legal affairs at that period. Because of the outbreak of war, I did nothing about it at the time; but some years later I wrote to the firm asking whether they had any old Fitzhugh records and, if so, whether I might call and examine them. One of the partners wrote back saying he would have been glad to let me do so, but unfortunately in the war their office had received a direct hit from a bomb, and all their papers had been destroyed. I kicked myself for not taking action sooner, and made a good resolution on promptness for the future. However, a little later I wrote to the Southampton Civic Record Office about some documents I wished to examine there. On my arrival, they had them ready for me, but the archivist said: 'And here, Mr FitzHugh, are some other records that I think will interest you.' He placed two large cardboard boxes in front of me and said: 'They come from a local lawyer's office.'

He went on to explain that right at the beginning of the war an appeal had gone out for salvageable material to be handed in for the war effort, including paper for recycling; and Page & Moody had patriotically answered the call. A corporation lorry was sent round to collect their contribution, and piles of old documents were carried out of the office and tossed on to it. That must have been at about one o'clock in the afternoon, because along the pavement came the city librarian on his way to lunch. Seeing documents being thrown on to the lorry, he climbed on to it to have a look. Reckoning some of them to be of interest to the city's history, he went in to the office, offered the salvage price for them and told the driver to deliver his load to the City Library.

The total hoard thus rescued consisted not only of old deeds, which many lawyers now deposit at record offices, but also of the correspondence appertaining to them. There were letters from my ancestors to Page & Moody's predecessors, and office copies of the solicitor's side of the correspondence, about a hundred Fitzhugh documents in all, revealing a great deal more than just legal matters, many and interesting though those were: my great-great-grandfather's movements to and from London, the breakdown of his mental health, the taking-over of his affairs by his wife and sons, and, from the signatures, the start in 1835 (evidently under the influence of the Gothic Revival) of the practice of spelling the Hugh in our surname with a capital letter.

*Land Tax records, mostly from 1780, throw light on the location of a family home in town or village, and the nature of the property they owned or occupied. In this one, Job Legg, a very small freeholder, assessed at 4s.0d, was the largest farmer of land in the parish at £31.17s.4d.*

County of Dorset to wit, for the Parish of Sutton Cheney in the said County. An Assessment made in Pursuance of an Act of Parliament passed in the 2d year of his present Majesty's Reign, for granting an Aid to his said Majesty by a Land Tax, to be raised in Great Britain, for the Service of the Year 1787

| Names of Proprietors | Names of Occupiers | Sums Assessed | | |
|---|---|---|---|---|
| | | £ | s | d |
| | John Stevens | 28 | 16 | 0 |
| The Revd. John Richards | Henry Legg | 25 | 1 | 4 |
| | Job Legg | 22 | 17 | 4 |
| | Henry Roberts | 7 | 18 | 8 |
| | The Revd. John Richards | 22 | 8 | 0 |
| Henry Legg | Henry Legg | 2 | 13 | 4 |
| William Coome | Job Legg | 3 | 4 | 0 |
| John Walbridge | Ditto | 5 | 12 | 0 |
| Job Legg | Do. | 0 | 4 | 0 |
| Charity School Land | Mr Kirkup | 0 | 7 | 2 |
| Charity Farm | Joseph Davis | 11 | 16 | 4 |
| Thomas Crofts | Thomas Crofts | 1 | 12 | 0 |
| John Bridge | Abel Brown | 0 | 10 | 8 |
| Elizabeth Turner | Thomas Ferrs | 1 | 14 | 0 |
| William Covens | William Covens | 2 | 5 | 4 |
| William Hansford | Sarah Baker | 5 | 6 | 8 |
| John Gladwyn | Ditto | 1 | 6 | 8 |
| Ditto | John Barge | 1 | 6 | 8 |
| Robert Ellis | Henry Legg | 1 | 4 | 0 |
| Francis Jno Brown Esqr | Levi Groves | 7 | 8 | 8 |
| John Howel | John Chappell | 1 | 4 | 0 |
| Mrs Long | Francis Stroud | 15 | 17 | 4 |
| the Revd. Mr Chaffin | Thomas Cox | 28 | 16 | 0 |
| George Bartlett | Francis Stroud | 4 | 12 | 0 |
| Charles Best Esqr | Joseph Hardy | 2 | 18 | 8 |
| John Brown | John Brown | 0 | 4 | 0 |
| Mary Hawkins | Mary Hawkins | 0 | 2 | 0 |
| | | £207 | 6 | 10 |

20th June 1787
Approved by us

R. Templeman

Wm Templeman

Nath. Templeman

Signed this 1st day of
June 1787 by us

John Gladwyn } Assessors
Job Legg }

## The ancestor as householder

Nearly all our Page & Moody papers were early nineteenth-century, but the oldest was a Deed of 1779 by which my ancestor of the previous generation contracted to rent a newly built house in Hanover Buildings Row, Southampton, for £36.15s a year. Among the jobs that the landlord undertook to do before he moved in were:

> Make a closet with shelves in the kitchen for the butler's pantry and fit up the kitchen with dresser with drawers and shelves, and also put bins in the cellar for wine; a place for coals and separations in the cellars (such separations to be made of lath and plaster at least), and also pave the wash house and fit the same up in a proper manner with pump, sink and drains; make a closet with shelves in the back parlour and two closets with shelves in each of the bed chambers; and also fit up neatly a necessary near the wash house, and fit up the necessary at the bottom of the garden for servants.

In the nineteenth century, large-scale Ordnance Maps, now reprinted, can help in locating a house; and in the middle of the century photography starts providing evidence. Some public libraries have collections of old photographic views and picture postcards of their area; but private photograph albums also come into the picture. They are largely filled with studio portraits of members of the family, but I have one of my family's home near Southampton in the 1850s. Rephotographed, and with no human figures to date it, it looks as though it was taken yesterday, and makes it hard to realise that the whole scene, the house, the trees and the garden, ceased to exist more than a hundred years ago.

My great-grandfather was a country clergyman. A rectory is one architectural feature of the rural landscape that seems to survive the rough winds of change even though the parson has moved to smaller premises and the building has become The Old Rectory, or the Glebe Guest House. I have a photograph, taken before 1882, of the one in Sussex in which my great-grandfather lived, and when I last saw it the building was quite unchanged.

If you have no photograph of an old family home that is still standing, you would be wise not to delay taking one. In these days, developers are everywhere. Having no photograph of the house where my grandfather lived in Bayswater, London, I went with a camera to take one. The whole street, I was glad to see, was obviously of his period, but I was dismayed to find that his house was now evidently a 'nightspot' catering for a clientele of undiscriminating taste, the porch being painted a violent purple. However, fearing that a tenancy so out of character with the rest of the street might imply a short lease pending demolition, I took my colour photograph of the house, and in my Family Transcripts volume a caption clears my grandfather of all responsibility for its appearance.

Now, from the location and exterior of ancestral homes to their interiors and contents. During the sixteenth and early seventeenth centuries there were certain specified chattels of which we can all feel pretty certain, since nearly every family, rich or poor, was obliged by law to keep them in the house. An Act of 1541 laid down:

> Every man being the King's subject, not lame, decrepit nor maimed nor having any other lawful or reasonable cause or impediment, being within the age of 60 years (except spiritual men, justices [etc.] shall . . . have a bow and arrows ready continually in his house to use himself . . . and that every man having a man-child in his house shall provide, ordain and have in his house for every man-child being of the age of 7 years till he shall come to the age of 17 years a bow and two shafts to induce and learn them and bring them up in shooting . . . and if the same young men be servants, that then their master shall abate the money that they shall pay for the same bows and arrows out of their wages.

The Will of William Fitzhugh who lived at the Green House, Bedford, mentioned the parlour in his house with its court-cupboard, long table and six high joint stools; but the most prolific record for revealing the contents of a long bygone home is the Probate Inventory. This document lists the movable effects of a deceased person, especially if he or she died intestate and Letters of Administration were applied for. It will have been drawn up by two reputable neighbours. In some cases the items are listed under the headings of the various rooms and outhouses in which they were found, thus adding greatly to its revelation of the ancestral home. Sometimes too, as already mentioned, the listing of equipment or stock in trade reveal the deceased's occupation.

These inventories are usually to be found at the same repository as the wills and other probate records, i.e. at the appropriate county record office or the Public Record Office, Chancery Lane. Few were made after 1750, though the only one I have found for my family just post-dates that half-century. However, it was contained not among probate records but as part of the papers of a Chancery suit. It was an inventory of furniture, kitchen equipment, clothing, wine, books, indoor games and other items that were the particular bones of contention between the brother and sister who were the litigants. They were articles also of very special interest to a family historian, namely 'six painted family pictures' identified as being

An Inventory of the goods and chattels [...]
of Hazellbery Brian who deceased the 6th day of November in the year
of our Lord 1706 taken and appraised [...]
[...]

<table>
</table>

| Imprimis | In the hall one [tableboard] four joint stooles three spetts one dreeppin pan two [...] with some other small things valued att | 00 — 13 — 04 |
| Item | In the kitchen four bras kettels four braspots [...] two graspans three skilletts two puter flagons sixteen puter dishes with some other small things valued att | 03 — 06 — 08 |
| Item | In the butrey four barrells two [...] one water[...] with some other lumber valued att | 00 — 10 — 08 |
| Item | In the Roome within the hall one [...] one settell two [...] to [...] with other things valued att | 00 — 06 — 08 |
| Item | In the Lodging chamber over the hall [...] two chests two coffers with some other small things valued att | 02 — 06 — 08 |
| Item | In the chamber over the kitchen one litell table one litell box one chest one [...] valued att | 00 — 07 — 00 |
| Item | for one horse one litell hayricke with some other lumber in the backside valued att | 03 — 05 — 00 |
| Item | for his wearing apparell valued | 01 — 00 — 00 |
|  |  | 11 — 16 — 00 |

Jurs of
Humprey Kelleman
Robart Hawkins

30. November 170[6]
[...]

Intimate information about the interiors of our ancestors' homes is revealed in probate inventories. Here the household chattels in the hall, kitchen, buttery, room within the hall, lodging chamber over the hall, and the chamber over the kitchen, are listed separately, a useful arrangement not always made.

portraits of their uncles (one of them my ancestor), their deceased brother, and maternal grandfather. Where, oh where, are those family portraits now? What would I not give to see them. Unfortunately for me, brother and sister came to a settlement out of court, leaving no clue as to who finally got what. Family portraits tend to pass down in the senior male line, but the brother's descendants died out. I fear those likenesses of my early eighteenth-century ancestor and his family have vanished for ever.

The items in a family inventory are worth rearranging to group like with like, e.g. all furniture together and separate from clothing, tools, etc. Such an arrangement tends to reveal aspects of the testator's character and tastes not immediately apparent in the next-come-next-noted order in which they were originally listed.

An Inventory, being a comparatively rare document, is a lucky find, but the main probate document, the Will, very often mentions personal articles selected as legacies. The Will of my ancestor's sister, Mary Rogers, in 1747 bequeathed yet more family portraits, miniatures this time, of her late husband, two brothers and a brother-in-law.

Finally, from the material contents of the house to its inhabitants other than the family. Until some two hundred years ago, the very word 'family' meant 'members of a household' and included any domestic staff. The fact that female servants once formed the largest single category of working women means that a very large section of the population employed them, not just the rich, as younger family historians of today tend to imagine. Even male servants were nothing unusual. Dickens was not being fanciful in giving the impecunious Micawbers their maid-of-all-work Clickett; and in Mrs Gaskell's *Cranford*, Miss Matty, who when she sat knitting alone of an evening could not afford to light more than one candle, had her Fanny. In many houses where domestic staff were employed, they might well constitute the majority of the household. Freedom from housework was the badge of gentility.

For family historians looking back beyond the census returns of 1841, systematic mentions of servants are limited to the poll tax levies of the seventeenth century (PRO, Chancery Lane under E.179), the Tax on Man Servants 1777-1882 and on Maid Servants 1785-92 at county record offices. In the Poll Tax Assessment of 1678, my hosier ancestor's household is shown as comprising:

William Fitzhugh senior, lodger for £100 money and for his poll.
William Fitzhugh junior.
His wife and 1 child.

This page from the 1851 Census Return includes three ordinary households with servants, one of them a manservant, showing how pervasive a role domestic staff played in the family life of past centuries. The children at 1 Butcher Row are obviously 'making their way' into professional life.

1 apprentice, Tho. Plates.
1 maid, Jane Jones, at £3 per annum.

A Man Servant Tax Assessment of 1780 shows the hosier's grandson, Valentine Fitzhugh, retired Turkey merchant, taxed for one manservant, who, as his grandson remembered, wore a green livery.

Apart from official records of domestic staff, mentions of their presence in a house are liable to occur in the type of lawsuits arising from internal family strife. In a suit in the Court of Star Chamber (STAC.8/108/1) in 1609, several of Robert Fitzhugh's servants, male and female, gave evidence of troubles in their employer's home. One of them, Joan Heath, told in her deposition how she had overheard a highly relevant conversation:

> Being making of a fire in the said Robert Fitzhugh's chamber in the time of his last sickness, [she] heard Elizabeth Fitzhugh complain unto her husband that his chest was rigged. And the said Robert Fitzhugh did ask her: 'By whom?' And the said Elizabeth did answer him: 'By your daughter [Anne] Cranwell, for', saith Mrs Fitzhugh, 'you have given her the key, as she saith, and have given her all that you have. And if you have done so', saith the said Elizabeth, 'I am undone, being a sick and aged woman'. Then the said Robert Fitzhugh swore: 'By God's blood, it is not so! I have given nothing from thee, neither will I', but said she should have all, and they that had anything should be beholden to her. And this deponent saith that there was none present at that time but this deponent and the said Elizabeth Fitzhugh.

Servants are often mentioned, by name or otherwise, in wills, especially women's wills. In 1784, the widow Mary Rogers, née Fitzhugh, whose spouse, a ship's husband (managing owner) of East Indiamen, had evidently left her comfortably off, made several bequests to her domestic staff (PCC, PROB.11/1164):

> I give all my wearing linen and apparel unto such servant who shall dress and wait upon me at the time of my decease. Also I give to my present coachman, William Curble, the sum of £100 over and above the wages which shall be due to him at the time of my decease. I also give to my present footman, John Price, the sum of £100 over and above the wages which shall be due to him at the time of my decease; but in case that either of them shall not be in my service at the time of my decease, the legacy to him who shall have quitted my service shall be void and not paid. I also give to

87

every servant who shall be in my service and shall have been so for seven years preceding my decease, not excluding the said William Curble and John Price, the sum of £20.

Another popular late-twentieth century illusion about those bygone extra-family members of the household is that they were all drudges working unreasonable hours for miserable wages. Some were of course, but that was not the norm. Their pay certainly was smaller than in other occupations, but that was because board and lodging came on top of it. Admittedly, too, they were on duty from the time they got up in the morning till the time they went to bed at night, but they were not working all that time; each one had his or her own tasks to perform. Mrs Rogers's long-serving staff must have been happy in their situations; and from my family's evidence in the next century, it is hard to picture their servants as drudges. In 1881 the family at Streat Rectory, Sussex, consisted of the 87-year-old parson and his two late-middle-aged daughters. To tend to their domestic needs they employed a cook, butler, laundress, under-laundress, lady's maid, housemaid, under-housemaid and kitchenmaid. No one can persuade me that those eight servants, even without modern labour-saving devices, lived other than a life of Riley.

*A family outing on the River Thames, complete with domestic staff, who were not always housebound drudges.*

The Clergy, Choir, Churchwardens, Clerk, and Sextons, 1863.

90

# 8

# The ancestor as public person

Here we consider ancestors holding posts of public responsibility at any level. The ones most likely to be encountered are those officiating in their home parish as churchwardens, vestrymen, overseers of the poor, surveyors of the highways, and petty constables. Most of the records of their activities have by now been deposited at the appropriate county record offices. They throw light on the lives of respectable local men carrying out their duties among and on behalf of their closest neighbours. In cities, the ward records of elected members and appointed officials administering their urban environment, are equally revealing. For the narrative family historian they tend to combine two important functions, providing an account of an ancestor's activities and setting him in his local context.

In 1634, William Fitzhugh, hosier, was appointed one of the two Stewards of the Wardmote Inquest of Bridge Ward Within, London. The meetings of this body at Fishmongers' Hall were governed by a number of rules, listed in *Records of Bridge Ward Within, MS 3461. Vol I*, many of which are identical with those for conducting meetings today, but the following selection will help the reader to form a mental picture of their proceedings:

2. *Not putting on of gowns* Item, if any of us do come in to the Questhouse and do not presently put on his gown, he shall pay, to the use of the poor, . . . . . . . . . . . . . . . . . . . . . . . . . . . . . . . . . . . . . . . .4d.
3. *Not keeping appointed hours* Item, if any of us shall be absent at the hours appointed (vizt) at eight in the morning and one in the afternoon by St Magnus' clock, he shall pay, to the use of the company, for every hour so offending without leave of the greater part, . . . . . . . . . . . . . . . . . . . . . . . . . . . . . . . . . . . . . . . . . . . . . .4d.
7. *Against gaming* Item, if any of us shall play at tables, dice, cards or any other game within the house during the time of our sitting, shall pay for every such offence, to the use of the poor, . . .6d.
8. *Against taking tobacco* Item, if any of us shall take tobacco in the Quest hall or near thereto, whereby the company or any other

> that shall come to us may be annoyed, shall pay to the general for
> every such offence, .....................................6d.
> 10.   *Needless courtesies* Item, if any of us shall put off his hat to any
> of the company, except it be at our coming in or going forth or
> desiring leave to depart in the time of our sitting, shall pay for
> every such offence, .....................................2d.

In April, three years later, my same ancestor became one of the three Overseers of the Poor for the southern section of his parish of St Olave's, Southwark. It was the duty of this official, under the authority of the Vestry, to assess the inhabitants for the poor rate, to collect it and spend it in relieving the needy. William Fitzhugh was unlucky when he took over the job that Easter, because plague was already rife in Southwark and the poor, because of their cramped living conditions, were the people most liable to infection. So bad was the situation a month later that, as described in *State Papers (Domestic), Vol.II*, the King's Council were moved to write to the JPs of the area, to whom the parochial authorities were responsible and who were in turn responsible to the King, as follows:

> Notwithstanding the great care taken by the Board for the relief of
> the poor infected persons in the parishes of Southwark ... there is
> no order observed in those parishes, especially in that of St
> Olave's, to separate the sick from those that are sound, nor to keep
> shut up houses where the contagion is. His Majesty is very sensible
> of this insufferable disorder, and if the justices take not a better
> course to suppress such disorders, the Lords will not consider
> them fit to hold the command His Majesty has reposed in
> them.

The trouble was that the poor rate was not raising enough money to deal with the exceptional numbers struck down. In spite of special measures to raise more, the end of William's year of office found him and his fellow overseers personally out of pocket.

   In 1666, William became Scavenger for the First Precinct of London Bridge (the section in Southwark). This was when the old bridge still bore houses and shops. His responsibility was the cleanliness of the roadway from the south bank as far as the drawbridge. The Southwark regulations itemised in *Presentments of the Guildable Manor, Southwark*, read:

> No person shall throw any piss out of their windows or any filth or
> dead dog or cat out of their doors or houses into the streets.

No person shall lay or cast into the streets any rubbish or earth but shall carry away the same within six hours.

Every inhabitant within this Manor shall sweep the street before their houses every day that the Raker cometh, and before he cometh, that the soil being laid together may be carried away. And that every Saturday, when the Raker is past, no more soil be cast out of their houses nor make any dung hill in the streets.

The Scavenger shall cause Rakers to cleanse the streets three days in every week, whereof Saturday chiefly to be regarded.

The Rakers shall upon every Tuesday, Thursday and Saturday (if it be not holiday) take away all such soil as shall be laid upon heaps or brought unto them.

The Scavengers, or one of them, shall every Saturday follow the Rakers' cart and see that the streets be well made clean and soil carried away.

'Earth' and 'soil' should not be confused; the latter was brought out from the houses' privies.

At that period, too, each male Londoner was subject to take his turn at the public duty of Watch, which obliged him to patrol certain streets at night under the superintendence of the local constable. In Southwark, as was laid down in the same record:

The Beadles of the Borough shall from time to time warn and charge so many of the inhabitants and housekeepers of this Borough to watch with the Constables of the night, as that there be a constant number of thirty complete Watchmen at the least every night to attend the Constables in their watch, and every day give to the Constable in writing a note of the names of such persons as he shall warn to watch the night following ...

Every Constable of the night watch shall cause the said thirty men so warned for the Watch to be placed at their several stages next hereafter mentioned, in this manner, vizt: two at Kent Street, three at St George's Church ... three at the Bridge Foot and five to attend the Constable for the night.

William Shakespeare had to pass through the Bridge Foot every time he went between his lodgings and the Globe Theatre; so the setting of the Watch by Dogberry and Verges in *Much Ado About Nothing* may be at least

# Disbursmts for ye Church 1733

## by Jas: Kellaway & John Bridle } Chhwardens

|  |  | £ | s | d |
|---|---|---|---|---|
| Imprimis Pd at Visitacon | | 0 | 2 | 0 |
| Itm Pd Will: Cull for work about ye Bells | | 0 | 1 | 6 |
| Gave to a Traveller with a Pass | | 0 | 0 | 6 |
| Gave ye Ringers 5th of Novemr | | 0 | 7 | 6 |
| Pd for Jubing a Bel | | 0 | 2 | 6 |
| Pd for Bread & Wine at Christmas | | 0 | 5 | 6 |
| 7br 29th 1733 Pd halfa Year's Gaolmoney & a Letter | | 0 | 19 | 0 |
| Pd for Lyme & Tyling ye Church | | 0 | 11 | 4 |
| Pd for work about ye Church house | | 1 | 5 | 6 |
| Pd Allen Dykes Bill | | 1 | 5 | 6 |
| March 25th 1734 Pd halfa Years Gaol money | | 0 | 18 | 9 |
| Pd for Wood for ye Glasier | | 0 | 0 | 6 |
| Pd Mr Mullet for Leather for ye Bells | | 0 | 5 | 0 |
| Pd Cull his whole Years wages | | 1 | 17 | 6 |
| Pd Cull for attending ye Glasier & other work | | 0 | 4 | 6 |
| Pd for Oyl for ye Bells | | 0 | 1 | 2 |
| Pd Jo: Hankins Bill | | 0 | 10 | 9 |
| Pd Mr Hill | | 0 | 11 | 10 |
| Pd Mr Loder | | 0 | 7 | 2 |
| Pd the Glasier's Bill | | 2 | 9 | 0 |
| Pd for Bread & Wine this Easter | | 0 | 5 | 6 |
| | | 12 | 12 | 0 |

| | £ | s | d |
|---|---|---|---|
| Collected 3 Rates & half | 19 | 19 | 9 |
| Disbursd | 12 | 12 | 0 |
| in | £ | 7 | 7 9 |

Apr 15th 17

Minister

a recognisable satiric picture of how the operation was carried out at that spot in practice.

In the last decade of the seventeenth century and first of the eighteenth, William's son was a vestryman of St Giles's, Camberwell, Surrey, and served at various times as Collector for the Poor and Surveyor of the Highways, and on a committee for re-allocating all the seats in the church. Then, in the 1720s and 1730s, his son Robert was a vestryman of St Peter's, Westcheap, London. For two years he was 'Mr Churchwarden', and in the Vestry Minute Books there are many accounts of the parish relief he distributed and the settlement problems he had to deal with.

The vestry and the offices connected with it may not be the only parochial records to throw light on an ancestor's local activities. Some urban parishes had their own schools, which have left minute books of their governors' meetings; and these throw interesting light on local conditions and the tasks allotted to individual governors. In my ancestor's year as churchwarden of St Olave's, Southwark, he became *ex officio* a governor of the parish's Grammar School, and later was appointed a regular governor. For many years he attended meetings both of its board and of the parish vestry. One example, culled from the *Minute Book of the Governors of St Olave's Grammar School*, of the human problems that came before him and his fellow governors, is a resolution taken at the first meeting they dared to hold after the Plague of London.

> Ordered that the residue of the quarterage due to Mr Bassill, the schoolmaster deceased, at Michaelmas last shall be paid to his wife when she leaves the house wherein she lives, provided she satisfy the milkwoman what is due to her before the money be paid.

In a very different sphere of life, the merchant service, all civil powers over the crew and passengers resided in the ship's captain. Each logbook and journal of a voyage is liable to mention instances of his exercise of penal power. The following is one example of the administration of punishment on the orders of Captain William Fitzhugh of the East Indiaman *Derby*:

> 1715, Monday 28th March ... At time of divine service Archibald Smith, seaman, was caught in Richard Savill's cabin stealing water, for which offence this morning brought him to the gangway, giving six lashes with cat-of-nine-tails.

*Churchwardens were the most senior of parochial officials. This list of James Kellaway and John Bridle's disbursements in 1733/ 34 shows the interesting variety of their responsibilities in a small village.*

## The ancestor as public person

The local newspapers of the nineteenth century carry many accounts of the meetings of voluntary bodies run by public-spirited people, such as, in the *Sussex Advertiser* of 31st July, 1860:

> East Sussex Book Hawking Association. The fifth annual meeting of this association was held at Lewes on the 24th inst, R.W. Blencowe, Esq. in the chair. The meeting was also attended by the Rev. W.A. FitzHugh, Rev. G.C. Shiffner, W. Slye, Esq. and several other gentlemen ... The report sums up the work of the association in the following terms: 'It has been the means of distributing the Word of God and the prayer book of the Church in great numbers. It has spread abroad and carried into the most unfrequented districts and to the most isolated homes a great variety of attractive and useful books, both secular and religious. And while thus encouraging the habit of reading among the people generally, it has tended also to foster in them a healthy spirit of honest independence by helping them to provide at their own cost and at a fair price a due supply of mental food for themselves and their families ...

A responsibility that was often undertaken by persons of recognised respectability was that of magistrate. In the 1880s my great-uncle Henry FitzHugh, on retirement from the army, became a Justice of the Peace. The cases that came before him were drawn from a more extensive area than those of a vestryman, and so give a wider, though still regional, picture of the world in which he lived. Cases reported in the local newspaper can be selected by the family historian to paint in the period background, or just to entertain his readers by reminding them how different life was in Queen Victoria's day. For instance, in 1887 he heard a case of drunken driving:

> William Banks was summoned for furious driving at Newhaven on the 28th February ... P.C. Suter stated that on the day in question about 3.45 he saw the defendant driving a two-wheeled cart over Newhaven Bridge. The horse was driven at a gallop, and, whilst passing over the rails, the cart nearly overturned and a child was nearly run over. He afterwards called on defendant at his house, and he was the worse for drink. The witness was cross-examined with the view of showing that the cart only jolted as it passed over the rails. Sergt Dibley corroborated the evidence of the constable but said he did not see anyone in danger. Mr Bedford called a lad named Reed who was sitting behind the cart and who denied that it had been furiously driven. The Bench fined defendant 1s and 17s 6d costs.

He might even reassure some readers who blame violence on television for what the young people of today are coming to:

> Thomas Cheame, a boy, was summoned for assaulting an aged woman named Sarah Longley at Seaford on May 19th [1887]. The complainant said she was 72 years of age. The defendant in the afternoon came to her house, burst the door open and threw stones into the house at her. She had suffered great annoyance from boys throwing stones into the house. They came about a dozen at a time. The Bench fined defendant 2s 6d including costs, which were reduced.

A public person is far more liable to be mentioned in records, both manuscript and print, than an entirely private person. So if ever one of your ancestors undertook any public duty, your chances of learning something about him and the social world around him will be greatly enhanced.

*Next in rank above parochial officials came the Justices of the Peace. Here a Justice examines William Frampton, who had become, or was liable to become, a drain upon parish rates. His past career was investigated to discover what parish was responsible for his relief. These settlement examinations are one of the most informative documents about the careers of working-class ancestors.*

97

# 9

# The ancestor among his contemporaries

In many a book of family history there is no more mention of the people among whom the ancestors spent their lives than if they had been the Swiss Family Robinson. With apparently no friends, enemies, neighbours, business associates or even nodding acquaintances, keeping themselves strictly to themselves, they pick their solitary way down the centuries and into these so-called 'histories'. Ancestors in aspic.

Actually, of course, once the researcher explores beyond mere genealogical evidence, almost all the data he finds are of the ancestor in some connection with his fellow men: his neighbours, his landlord, his employer, his apprentice, his friends, the enemy who sues him, etc. Social interactions made up not his whole life, but almost all we are likely to discover. Exclude them from your history and what have you left? The family tree! Which is where you started.

In the chapter on research I stressed the importance of transcribing much more than bare references to named members of the family. Anything and anyone mentioned in each of the circumstances in which they appear should be noted. It is from such liberal transcripts that repeated mentions of the same person can come to light. Some of these may indicate that the person and the ancestor were more than merely locally associated. His name may also occur on a marriage certificate as witness to the wedding. This can point to a close friendship, though it is worth looking to make sure his name does not keep recurring at other people's weddings, showing that he was signing *ex officio* as verger or parish clerk. If a person's name occurs in an ancestor's will as executor or overseer, he will obviously have been a trusted friend (or occasionally a creditor); but if he appears merely as witness, he may have been no more than someone conveniently on the spot, such as a servant, neighbour or lawyer's clerk.

Comparison of some liberally transcribed records with others may show that the John Brown who lived next door but one to your ancestor

*Friendly Societies flourished in the nineteenth century to provide funds for members who fell on hard times. The picture shows the range of social classes involved, as indicated in part by their headwear.*

was in the same, or an allied, occupation, shared the same political opinions and discussed parochial affairs with him at vestry meetings. If, for some reason, he earns a mention in your family history, these items of knowledge can enable you to make him more than just a name.

If you are lucky enough to have a family wedding reported in a nineteenth-century local newspaper, you will discover a whole circle of friends and relations of both parties in the list of invited guests.

In the narrative history I am writing, my running index contains far more names of 'outsiders' than of members of the family. It includes people my ancestors never met or even wanted to meet, but whose activities impinged upon their lives. Business activities are subject to influences from all sorts of unexpected quarters. The account I have written of the import/export trade carried on by William Fitzhugh (1717-83), who was a factor in Aleppo for the Levant Company, involved mention of notables in Turkish political history:

> Early the following May 1749, Giorgio Aidé [the factory's dragoman] and William Fitzhugh, joined now by John Free, fitted out a second caravan to take trade goods to Persia via Baghdad. The rest of the factors still hung back and this time with better reason. There was unrest in southern Mesopotamia; the Pasha of Basra was in revolt against the Sultan and rumoured to be threatening Baghdad . . . The camel caravan, carrying 300 bales of cloth, indigo and other goods, set off under the direction of an Armenian employee of Aidé's called Ohan Zadur . . . On arrival at Baghdad, the bales were taken into the Custom House to await the agent to whom Aidé had consigned them, an Armenian called Yakub Gian who lived at Basra. So far, all had gone as well as the time before, but now everything began to go seriously wrong.
>
> Solyman, the rebellious Pasha of Basra, was attempting to blockade Baghdad, and this delayed Gian's arrival. Baghdad had its janissary force, but the Governor, Pasha Hajji Mehemet, having no money to pay them with, was fearful of their going over to the enemy. However, being a Pasha of three tails and therefore of the highest authority, he did not balk at commandeering the contents of the Custom House and selling them for the wherewithal to pay his men. He legitimised the measure by issuing bonds to the dispossessed owners for a conservative estimate of their cost price; so that when Yakub Gian reached the city to market the goods, all that was there for him was a bond for 69,000 dollars, and it was all made out to Giorgio Aidé, the only owner whom Ohan Zadur had mentioned.

This confiscation of William Fitzhugh's trade goods led on to still more interesting consequences, imperilling even the career of the British Ambassador at Constantinople.

Even the mental compromises and conflicts of conscience that the Restoration of 1660 imposed on William Fitzhugh (1599-1679) became manifest to me only through his connections with his fellow parishioners. He had been a supporter of Parliament against the King and of Puritanism against the Anglican church, and as such, he and the other Governors of St Olave's Grammar School who had been appointed during the Civil War and Interregnum were faced at the Restoration with the need for some radical rethinking. As public officials they now had to subscribe to the Oaths of Allegiance and Supremacy, acknowledging Charles II as King and head of the Church. On the evidence of the *Minutes of the Governors' Meetings*, I wrote:

> However, William and all his fellow Governors felt able to subscribe —but with one possible exception. The parish's pre-war leader against Anglicanism, tavern-keeper Cornelius Cooke, had failed to attend any Governors' Meeting since the King's return. So when, on 11th January 1661, Cooke was again absent, Edmund Warnett and William [Fitzhugh], Cooke's next-door neighbour, were deputed to call on him at the Bear Inn and put the question whether he conceived himself still to be in a capacity of sitting as a member of the Court or not. The answer Cooke gave them, probably not without reproaching them as turncoats, was that he conceived himself 'uncapable' and therefore did refuse to sit in the Court. On receiving this intimation, the next meeting proceeded to the election of a new Governor, and the old Puritan was replaced by Lt-Colonel George Moore.

It is hardly possible now to gain any real inkling into our forerunners' lives or characters except through connections with the people among whom they lived their lives; so to write about them without mentioning these neighbours and others amounts to a more or less deliberate process of isolation.

There is one particular group of contemporaries who are likely to be of special importance to an ancestor, namely his in-laws. Once a man is married, his wife's family tend to play almost as large a part in his life as do his own. What has been said under Research about the roles of an ancestor's siblings therefore applies also to some extent to his in-laws. By the time an ancestry researcher decides to take off from genealogy into family history, he will almost certainly have already discovered his

*A marriage means the accession, to both bride and bridegroom, of a whole new set of relations. Walter Rawcliffe, at his marriage in Fallowfield, Manchester, in 1883, here gains six new brothers and sisters-in-law (ringed).*

ancestresses' ancestors. Now he must find her siblings and parents' siblings, any one of whom is liable to appear as a character of some importance in his family story. I have found this happen again and again in my family, as the following examples show.

1.  William Fitzhugh (1599-1679) married Mary Smith. In 1640 he took on her young brother Nathaniel as his apprentice and later as junior partner. Nathaniel married and had three daughters. One of them married a Captain in the East India Company's merchant marine who took William Fitzhugh's grandson, his wife's first cousin once removed, to sea as midshipman in 1703. Another of Smith's daughters married and had a daughter, who, when the midshipman became a captain in 1713, married him and became my ancestress.

2.  Captain Fitzhugh's son Valentine was in business as a factor for the Levant Company in Istanbul. There he married the young Huguenot Elizabeth Palmentier. When he was thinking of retiring to England in 1762 he needed to find a partner to continue his business. He chose his brother-in-law, Elizabeth's brother William Palmentier.

3.  Valentine's son William married Charlotte Hamilton. Charlotte had a cousin who controlled the 24-elector parliamentary pocket borough of Tiverton in Devon. When a new member was needed for the constituency in 1803 and the cousin's son was only a child, William was offered the seat and kept it warm for fifteen years until the heir came of age.

4.  In the next generation, my reverend ancestor's mother-in-law was patron of the living of Streat in Sussex and appointed him to it in 1821; and there he spent the rest of his life.

So the nearest relations of each ancestress should be sufficiently researched for you to recognise their fingers in the family pie. From the point when an ancestress first appears among my family records, which may be on the day of the wedding, I treat her relations in much the same way as sisters' husbands, noting anything about their activities likely to impinge upon the main characters of my story, namely my ancestors, ancestresses and ancestors' siblings. If, in some of the instances just cited, the relationships that lay behind their interposition had not been realised, a great deal of the true significance of the ancestor's career would have been missed.

A title often chosen by writers of biographies is *The Life and Times of (What's-his-name)*, and it seems to be specially favoured when the subject is a man or woman about whom the known personal facts are not plentiful enough to fill a volume by themselves. All biographies — and family histories are of course a linked series of biographies — do their best to place their subjects firmly in their social background, and this is possible only by surrounding them with their contemporaries.

*The advent of motorised transport meant the possibility of 'works outings', usually photographed. If your ancestor worked for Bird & Pippard's of Yeovil when the charabanc visited Cheddar Gorge, this photograph probably shows him amongst his workmates and contemporaries.*

*The growth of Britain's overseas trade led many ancestors to work abroad for chartered companies whose archives now record their lives in fascinating detail. In the eighteenth century, the British taste for tea made that commodity the most important import from Asia. This picture from 'Johnson's England' shows a London tea-merchant's card.*

# 10

# The ancestor as expatriate

This chapter deals with Britons travelling or working abroad but domiciled in Britain, not with emigrants who settled permanently overseas, leaving the evidence of their careers in the archives of the United States, Canada, Australia, New Zealand, South Africa and other countries once shown pink on the map of the world. When I set out on my searches I was already aware that in the eighteenth century three generations of my family had spent their working lives abroad, so I assumed that that period was going to prove a lean one in my narrative history. I could not have been more wrong.

Of Britons working abroad before about 1800, perhaps the majority were employees of various chartered companies. Such organisations were founded on the strength of royal charters granting them a monopoly of British trade to certain defined regions of the world. This exclusiveness is helpful to us today because it means that if you have any evidence or tradition connecting a member of your family with a certain area of the world you can feel pretty confident that he was there as a servant of the appropriate company, and if his company traded to Asia or the Middle East you are likely to be extremely fortunate.

The greatest of all the chartered trading organisations was the Honourable East India Company, incorporated in the year 1600 with a monopoly of English trade to lands bordering the southern seas from the Cape of Good Hope eastwards to Cape Horn. It steadily increased in wealth and power until it ruled India. Evidence of the lives of thousands of traders, civil servants and seamen are housed in the enormous archives of the India Office Library and Records at Orbit House, Blackfriars Road, London SE1. The working lives of these enterprising men were always interesting and often exciting. They are contained in the minutes, correspondence and accounts of the Company's headquarters in London, in the business diaries and letters of its trading stations in the East, and in its ships' journals. A man's career can often be followed from the day he entered 'John Company's' service till he retired or died in harness. Also, if one member of a family was employed in the company, there is a strong likelihood that he was not the only one. Since the prospects for making money were exceptional, the inside influence of relations or friends was the surest method of gaining admittance ahead of other applicants. Also, once the company servants retired home to Britain, they and their womenfolk are likely to be found linked in a close marital network with other members of the Company.

The India Office Library and Records has published a *Brief Guide to Biographical Sources*, which is available from Orbit House. There is also an article by myself on 'East India Company Ancestry' in the *Genealogists' Magazine*, vol.21, no.5. In addition to the Company's manuscript records, the library of printed books contains valuable background material for the family historian.

The traders to the Middle East were incorporated in the Worshipful Company of Merchants of England Trading to the Levant Seas, usually called the Levant (or Turkey) Company and its members Turkey Merchants, because, throughout its existence from the sixteenth to the early nineteenth century, the countries around the eastern Mediterranean to which it traded were all realms of the Ottoman Empire, ruled by the Sultan of Turkey. The records of this company are nothing like as extensive as those of its counterparts for the East Indies, but often more than sufficient for an interesting account of an ancestor's career in the Middle East. The organisation of the company differed from that of the East Indies and gave rise to files of correspondence from the factors abroad to their principals in London, and these throw intimate light on their problems and opinions. The letters, Minute Books and other records of the factories, together with relevant correspondence of the British Ambassador at Constantinople, are housed at the Public Record Office, Chancery Lane, under *State Papers*, and have been catalogued by the List and Index Society. The Hertfordshire County Record Office holds the papers of the Radcliffe family of Turkey merchants; and another collection is in the private ownership of the Bosanquet family at Dingestow Court, Gwent. It is advisable to start by reading A.C. Wood's *A History of the Levant Company* (1935) and Ralph Davis's *Aleppo and Devonshire Square* (1967).

Britain's eighteenth-century wars had only minor effects on the daily lives of the civilian population at home, but for ancestors overseas engaged in the import/export business the progress of hostilities could be of vital importance. During the War of the Austrian Succession (1741-8) the superiority of the Royal Navy and British privateers over the French in the Mediterranean caused jubilation to William Fitzhugh at Aleppo, because destruction of the enemy's merchant fleet eliminated their competition and so increased his sales; but to his brother Valentine at Constantinople the effect was alarm and despondency. The holds of many of the French merchant ships captured by the British were filled with the cargoes of neutral Turkish traders. These innocent sufferers clamoured to their government to reimburse them by confiscating the assets of British residents in Constantinople, a threat that Valentine and his colleagues had constantly to fend off by raising loans to compensate them.

The business records of these companies are by no means confined to commercial transactions that readers of your family history might find dull. There were frequent political disputes, some of them dangerous, with the officials of the country in which the company's agents were living; and some of the recorded incidents were entirely of a personal nature. One of these caused me to disturb the quiet of the reading-room when it was in King Charles Street by laughing out loud. In 1776, Mr George Rogers, a member of the Company's Council at Canton, was outraged by the conduct of a newcomer, 19-year-old William Fitzhugh, the factory's most junior clerk. He reported him to the Council:

> As I was walking to my rooms, I saw Mr Fitzhugh in the factory ... After I had made the proper compliments, Mr Fitzhugh turned from me a little space and made water. I asked him if he was accustomed to do so in the factory. He answered: 'No, faith, only sometimes.' Upon which I could not help saying I thought it was a dirty trick. He immediately came and asked me what I meant by a dirty trick; that I was a dirty fellow for saying so. He further said he would not further expose me in the factory but would go with me to Whampoa tomorrow [a coded challenge to a duel]. Upon which I replied that I did not look upon myself on a footing with him but much his superior. He again called me a dirty fellow and a poltroon, which so irritated me that I called him a scoundrel. He then collared me and struck me with his cane several blows, which not choosing to return in the middle of the factory, I told the coolies to desist from the business they were upon with Mr Fitzhugh and likewise told him I should acquaint Mr Wood of what happened, which I soon afterwards did.

Repercussions naturally followed, and William nearly lost his job.

For the leisure activities of Britons working in the Middle East, glimpses are provided by the numerous travellers to Asia Minor who published accounts of their experiences. These also supply the family historian with a superabundance of background material. Alexander Drummond, in his book of *Travels* to various countries, describes one expedition he made in 1747:

On the 17th August last, the Reverend Mr Hemmings, Mr Fitzhugh, Mr Levett, Mr Chitty and I took our departure from Aleppo equipped with everything necessary for a journey through the deserts of Arabia and other countries inhabited by savages ... Having decamped from the banks of the Aphreen, we crossed that river in our way toward Corus, but before we reached this place were insolently stopped at a paltry hut-village by a posse of Gourdins who ... swore we should not pass unless we would gratify them with money, brandy and tobacco. A council of war being instantly called, it was determined that we should make our way good, although they were double our number. They were made acquainted with our resolution, upon which they ran to arms ...

Another great chartered company whose records survive is the Hudson's Bay Company of fur traders in Canada. Though the records are in Canada, there are microfilm copies at the Public Record Office, Kew, Surrey; but permission to search them has to be obtained from Hudson's Bay & Annings Ltd, 77 Main Street, Winnipeg, Manitoba, Canada R3C 2R1.

To turn from east to west: the Seven Years' War of 1756-63 resulted in the accession by Britain of a number of colonial possessions, and these led to opportunities for British investment, of which William Fitzhugh, retired home from Aleppo, took advantage by purchasing a sugar plantation in St Vincent in the West Indies. To research the contemporary background of the island to which he travelled, I perused the printed series of *State Papers (Colonial)*. In Volume IV I found:

The Island of St Vincent is about 25 English miles in length and 15 broad. In general mountainous and hilly ... It is in part possessed by wild Caribs and negroes, supposed to be from four to five thousand in number, who consider themselves to be, and really are, an independent people, very jealous of any settlement by Europeans upon this island, which they look upon as their own property. Several settlements have, however, at different times been made established by the French, who are computed to amount to about thirteen hundred souls, employing about three thousand four hundred negro slaves and having a considerable quantity of sheep, horned cattle and beasts of labour; the chief of their produce is cocoa, coffee and tobacco ...

The plantation that William bought in 1763 remained in the family for a

CANE-HOLEING.

*Slaves on a West Indian sugar plantation. Though Britain abolished its slave trade in 1807, slave labour was the source of much of her imported wealth until the Emancipation Act (1833) came into full force in 1838.*

hundred years, but the slaves who worked it were freed in 1838. To ensure that no new slaves were bought after the abolition of the trade in 1807, a register of those on each plantation was taken from time to time, and these are now at Kew in Treasury class T.71. They show, among the information for each slave, whether he or she had been brought over from Africa in the infamous Middle Passage, or was descended from earlier enforced emigrants, in which case they were described as Creoles. The alphabetical lists made for our family's plantation in 1817 began as follows:

### List of Male Slaves belonging to Richmond Vale Estate

| Names | Colour | Employment | Age | Country |
|---|---|---|---|---|
| Abraham | Negro | Carpenter | 28 years | Creole |
| Adam | Do. | Labourer | 14 do. | Do. |
| Alexy | Do. | Stock Keeper | 21 | Do. |
| Andrew | Do. | Infant | 4 | Do. |
| . . . . . | | | | |

111

and of female slaves:

| Adelaide | Negro | Infant | 7 months | Creole |
|---|---|---|---|---|
| Abigail | Do. | Superannuated | 80 years | Do. |
| Amelia | Do. | Labourer | 34 Do. | African |
| Angel | Mulatto | Washer | 50 | Creole |

For Britons travelling abroad before the First World War, it was not necessary to hold a passport. The first, optional documents of this description were as much letters of introduction as anything else. They were issued for each foreign journey and usually mentioned the traveller's country of destination. Once a traveller reached that destination and wished to return home or go on somewhere else, a further passport might be obtained from the British embassy or consulate. If a family were travelling together, the passport was likely to name only the husband/father, who would be in charge of the party.

During the short-lived peace with Napoleon of 1801-3, my great-great-grandfather took his family to France. The passport issued to him was recorded at the Foreign Office as:

*Date*: 1802 June 18
*No*: 341
*Names*: Mr Fitzhugh and family
*Where going*: France
*By whom recommended*: Mr Richard Grosvenor
*Stamp*: 2.2.6.    2 [shillings]

The *Register of Passports* (FO.610) is at the Public Record Office, Kew. It starts from 1795 and is entered in chronological order. There are, however, *Indexes of Names* to it (FO.611) for the periods 1851-62 and 1874-98. The present type of book passport containing a photograph of the holder was introduced in 1921.

Cross-Channel travellers arriving at and leaving Boulogne between 1822 and 1858 had their movements recorded among the *Archives Communales* of the Pas-de-Calais at Arras, as described in an article by Brian V.J. Maringo in the *Genealogists' Magazine*, Vol.22, No.5. And records of entering and leaving France can be found among the archives of the French départements where the crossings of the frontier were made.

My ancestor's widowed sister, Mary Lance, died in France and the record of her burial there was obtained at the Public Record Office, Chancery Lane, London. Under *Miscellaneous Registers of Deaths and Burials Abroad* (RG.33/60/89a), the information it provided was:

*Certificate of Burials*

Burials performed in the City of Paris and its Environs and entered in the Register kept by the Chaplain to the British Embassy at the court of France in the year 1835.

| Names | Abode | When Buried | Age | By whom the ceremony was performed |
|-------|-------|-------------|-----|-----------------------------------|
| Mary Lance | Paris | March 23rd | 74 | M.H. Luscomb, Bishop |

There are other registration records of 'foreign' births, marriages and deaths at the Public Record Office under RG.32-36. The Guildhall Library, London, also holds a number of registers of similar 'vital' events abroad, as does the General Register Office, but these last mostly concern men in the armed services.

A ship taking an ancestor, whether as passenger or member of the crew, to a far distant destination such as India, China, Australia or New Zealand, will have had to put in at ports of call on the way for fresh water and provisions; and in the days of sail, periods spent in port waiting for a wind or a new moon could be very protracted. So some description of these places adds conviction to the story of the voyage. From the beginning of the eighteenth century, books of travel were numerous and provide interesting accounts of the main ports of the sea-faring world. In *The Present State of the Cape of Good Hope* (1731) Peter Kolb wrote of Cape Town:

> The streets, the courtyards, the houses and everything in 'em are kept (as is the manner of the Dutch) extremely neat and clean. The houses are of stone, but most of 'em only one story. None are of more than two, and this on account of the violence of the easterly winds ... There were formerly shelving penthouses erected on both sides the streets to shelter the passengers in rainy weather ... Sailors and Hottentots were continually crowding and smoking their pipes under them and sometimes, through carelessness, set them on fire. The government laid hold of that occasion to rid the streets of the crowds of those fellows ... by publishing an order ... that no Hottentot or common sailor should smoke in the streets, with a declaration that the sailor or Hottentot who should presume to do so should be tied to the whipping-post and severely lashed with a rope-end on his bare posteriors.

Sometimes it was the ship's presence in port that was the cause of interesting incidents. On the eastward route, British ships called at the

Easter Sunday beautiful day service 3 times on the ____ the Bishop preached he seems a very nice man ____ ____ ____ ____ very ____ ____ some handles ____ ____ ____ don't swear he enjoyed poor boy ____ ____ ____ ____ thing ____ ____ it is sad to see one ____ ____ and something for him to try on and ____ ____ ____ ____ ____ here to ____ whilst in the ____ ____ ____ ____ and the ladies are very ____ ____ ____ ____ early ____ young men next berth ____ ____ ____ ____ ____ ____ all the way but there ____ ____ ____ ____ they are so many we go low ____ knots ____ ____ in the ____ side of the Cape of Good Hope ____ ____ going ____ ____ to see it ____ ____ ____ ____ and rainy ____ ____ ____ ____ desperate ____ we are going ____ knots an hour ____ ____ fine ____ ____ ____ ____ ____ and there ____ ____ tremendous sea ____ ____ and all movables were ____ ____ ____ George ____ the same ____ ____ restless ____ we have ____ ____ ____ below stairs I generally go but ____ ____ ____ ____ ____ ____ boxes ____ people ____ ____ some ____
Wednesday 5 ____ ____ very rough night ____ iceberg seen ____ ____ ____ of sea ____ ____ under several inches deep ____ ____ ____ ____ ____ night the Captain fell and broke his ____
Thursday ____ ____ another rough night some are highly ____ at the thing and ____ ____ ____ ____ the ____ cold George ____ ____ cheerful ____ night ____ to Mother about ____ ____ ____ ____ ____ ____ ____ ____ ____ went ____ ____ ____ ____ ____ the same ____ and asked him ____ ____ as I could he had been in bed all day since ____ ____ ____ ____ and had got such a way of ____ ____ ____ when he wanted nothing which ____ ____ ____ ____ ____ he said he wondered that night ____ ____ ____ presently he was ____ ____ he ____ ____ nothing fell asleep again and was awoke ____ Mother telling me ____ ____ was dying ____ ____ ____ saw her ____

*The adult lives of British emigrants lie recorded overseas, but letters describing their early adventures and privations are treasured possessions in many families. Using pages of writing-paper twice, in the manner here shown, kept the cost of postage down. The following extract from this long letter is from Anne Cutforth, a passenger on the 'Mermaid', en route to Australia in 1855.*

*Wednesday 25th. has been a very rough night, an iceberg seen early but out of sight in 5 minutes. Water several inches deep on deck, rough at night. The captain fell and broke his collar bone.*

*Thursday 26th. had another rough night. Some are highly amused at the time and bottles rolling about. It is very cold. George seemed very cheerful at night, talked to mother about Melbourne, wished we were there. Tucked him up before I went. I slept in an under bed the same berth and asked him to be as still as he could. He had been in bed all day since the cold weather came and had got such a way of calling 'mummy' or 'Annie' when he wanted nothing, which often distracted mother when it was needless. He said he would try that night. I fell asleep. Awoke presently — he was making a noise, he said he wanted nothing. I fell asleep again and was awoke by mother telling me George was dying.*

*I got up and saw he was much changed. A friend who knew something about the case came — said he was sinking as fast as he could. We knew the doctor could do no good. Somebody called him but he did not hear. The second mate called the chaplain. When mother came to him as she did every night, many times, he asked for a drink but could not take it, by which she knew he was worse, as he was always so eager for drink. She said she would not leave him. He pressed her hand, smiled, but could not speak. It would be 3 when mother woke me. I spoke to him, he seemed to try to speak, but could not and never did again. He was past noticing when the chaplain came. He stayed with us till all was over, prayed and spoke beautifully to us.*

*Presently poor George seemed to revive — he had laid with his eyes fixed but then seemed to look about a little; but he had begun some time to breathe hard and rattle in his throat. Mother gave him a little wine and water with a spoon; he swallowed some, but as he took the last a fearful struggle came and it was fearful to see. I shall never forget the sight. Then a breath or two and it was all over. He was dead. It was ten minutes past 5, 27th April.*

*The Mermaid*

East India Company's staging-posts, so once the date of a ship's arrival has been ascertained from her logbook and journal the records of the local factory should be consulted. I have found cases, not always mentioned in the ship's journal, of fighting, rape and murder by members of the crew ashore, drunken passengers getting left behind, stowaways being found, and incidents in which an ancestor was personally involved. For example, on 15th June 1716 at the island of St Helena the *St Helena Factory Minutes* record:

> The Governor says ... a boat went from on board the *Derby* to the West Rocks and stayed some small time. Upon which, the Guard going to see what they did, the boat put off; and [the Guard] found there landed 10 gunny bags containing 130 pieces of blue cloth and a parcel of chintz, which the Governor ordered to be brought within the Castle ... The Captain [Fitzhugh], appearing, says that he owns the blue cloth to be his, but knows nothing of the chintz; and he says 'tis his coxwain's fault and mistake, not for the lucre of saving the Custom but because he could not land them so conveniently as where he did, as he told him since.
>
> The Governor says the coxwain told him that he had orders to land the goods there and could as well have landed them at the usual landing place; which is very likely to be true because he brought the Company's rice in the same boat and put it ashore at the crane and then went above a mile off to land those goods
> . . .

I am afraid it was a pretty clear case against the Captain of smuggling and trying to lie his way out. Whitewash is no part of a family historian's stock in trade. My ancestor was fined, but his career was in no way affected.

After citing two instances of misconduct by Fitzhughs abroad, allow me to offset any unfavourable impression of the family by quoting 'Our Special Correspondent with General Roberts' from a yet unidentified newscutting pasted into an album. The all-too-common practice of preserving these cuttings without the name or date of the newspaper is most frustrating.

In the Second Afghan War (1878), when the British were aiming to keep Russian influence out of Kabul, my great-uncle Alfred, of the 5th Gurkhas, was bringing up the rearguard of our advancing troops when he and his men were surrounded by an Afghan force in the Chappri Defile. After describing the ambush, the war reporter concluded:

> Major Fitzhugh behaved in the most gallant manner. The camel

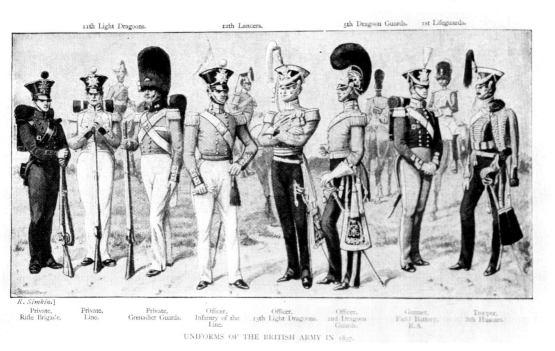

*Numerous illustrated books on military uniforms offer opportunities to find one of a relevant regiment and date for an army ancestor.*

drivers had bolted; so had the dhoolie bearers. He made his own men lead the camels and carry the dhoolies. He then moved with the remainder of his regiment steadily and slowly along, seeing every particular of baggage safely before him. The Mongols gibbered, yelled and shot at the line from every side; but the Gurkhas never broke. For that trying march Major Fitzhugh deserves the Victoria Cross if ever man did. He saw every camel safely into camp that night. The Mongols were frustrated in getting an ounce of plunder except what they got in the shape of cold lead. This was all through the patient pluck of Major Fitzhugh and his splendid little men.

Alfred FitzHugh was not awarded the VC, but did finish the campaign as a Companion of the Bath. Army records, newspaper war correspondence and military memoirs are fruitful sources of information about ancestors or their siblings serving abroad, and by their very nature often contain exciting incidents to enliven the family history.

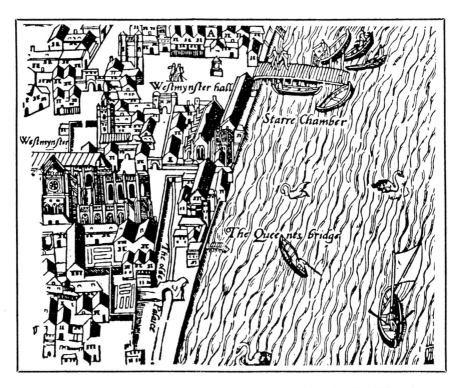

Ralph Aggas' map of London includes the Starre Chamber by Westminster
Hall in 1633, just before it was closed.

# 11

# The ancestor as litigant

In the middle of our consideration of basic ancestral aspects the reader now finds himself facing a chapter heading with a decidedly marginal look, and he may conclude that the bottom of the barrel is about to be scraped. Nothing could be further from the mark. We have just arrived at the richest of all mines of intimate family revelations.

The legal disputes in which our ancestors became involved can be discovered among the records of the central equity courts, namely those of Star Chamber, Requests (both closed in 1642), Exchequer and Chancery. The accusations of the plaintiffs and the denials or justifications of the defendants are all available for perusal at the Public Record Office, Chancery Lane, London, accompanied sometimes by the evidence given by witnesses and details of how the suits progressed and ended.

Extant Bills of Complaint and Answers in the Court of Chancery alone, down to the year 1875, amount to 19,000 bundles, each containing on average seventy cases, making more than a million in all. It has been said that any family owning any real estate will almost inevitably have been concerned in a Chancery case at some time or other; and that must surely be true, because I have come upon no less than fourteen cases in which my particular branch of my own family has been involved, either as plaintiffs or defendants. In addition to those fourteen Chancery suits, the same branch of the family features once in the Court of Requests, once in the Exchequer Court and twice in Star Chamber. Doubtless all those eighteen disputes were a great worry to my ancestors and ancestresses, but how thankful I am for them now.

Cases in the equity courts were largely concerned with money, land, business contracts, and inheritances. All are of interest to the family historian, but none more so than those in which the plaintiffs and defendants were members of the same family or their in-laws. Depositions (spoken evidence of witnesses taken down in writing by officials commissioned by the court) and answers given under interrogation often reveal intimate family and household details, bygone business practices, and the quoted words of conversations.

Many of the cases concern single incidents of dissension, but others arise out of circumstances that have continued over years and throw light over more than one generation of a family. The immense value of these records for family history purposes seems surprisingly little appreciated, or the Public Record Office would surely have included an account of them in its *Tracing Your Ancestors in the Public Record Office*. However, one of the PRO's free leaflets does deal with Chancery court records.

To illustrate the sometimes breathtaking amount of family information to be found in a single equity court record, I have picked two examples from my own family's legal disputes. First, one that shows how much a case can reveal about decades of the lives of two generations.

In 1754 Anne Hassard, née Fitzhugh, and her husband brought a suit against her brother William Fitzhugh on account of their father's will. I have extracted the following wording straight out of Anne's Bill of Complaint, combined with William's Answer (*Chancery Proceedings* C.11/ 1120/25); but to make them readable here I have dropped the legalistic identifying of everyone, every time his name is repeated, as 'the said' (e.g. 'the said Robert Fitzhugh', 'the said Defendant'), and also the repetition of their names always in full. Otherwise it is an abstract from the recorded text:

> By Articles of Agreement of or about 19th May 1714, Robert Fitzhugh did covenant that if his wife Margaret should die in his lifetime leaving two or more children living, that then Robert's executors should within three months pay to such children so much as would make their respective part £500 apiece.
>
> Robert Fitzhugh carried on the trade of a linendraper in Cornhill and afterwards in Cheapside, and he and Margaret, his wife, had several children, and all such, other than the Complainant [Anne] and Defendant [William], died in the lifetime of their father and mother unmarried and without issue. And in or about the year 1727 Robert Fitzhugh and John Barton did agree to become partners together in the trade of linendraper from the 25th December 1727 for the term of ten years ...
>
> William was educated by his father [Robert] in a manner fit for an apprentice and not otherwise. He believes his late father and John Barton at the beginning of their co-partnership did make large and considerable profits and advantages, but he has heard his father and John Barton did not for some years before the dissolution make so much advantage as they had formerly done ... And they continued in partnership until some time in

or about the month of December 1738 and by Indenture [then dissolved the partnership with full financial details given]. And John Barton, at the request of Robert Fitzhugh, without any consideration paid to him, [did] take William to be his apprentice in the trade and business for seven years ...

And William did continue as such for six years and ten months or thereabouts, when his father, growing to a time of life when he proposed to have declined and left off trade in favour of his son, to his mortification perceived from many instances in the conduct of his son that he was very remiss and averse to that trade and business and declared he would not carry them on, but requested his father to purchase a place for him in some military employment; but his father was very unwilling to do so, as knowing his business was much more beneficial and profitable; and therefore, to wean and persuade his son from his intended purpose and to induce his more close attention to his trade, declared to his son his intention of quitting his trade in his favour. But William, persisting in his inclination to the army, disregarding his fathers admonitions, by his ill conduct contracted several considerable debts, for some of which he was arrested, which was a great grief to his father, who was obliged to pay his debts to save him from gaol.

Fearing William would not be reclaimed, Robert was forced to comply with his son's request and purchased a commission of an ensign of foot in Hopkinson's Regiment [sic], then on the Irish establishment, and paid £300 upwards for the same. And within the year William embarked for America and continued there for two years or thereabouts, when the regiment returned to Ireland; and soon after his arrival in Ireland, which was in September 1749, his mother did remit to him £20.

William afterwards applied to his father to purchase for him a further promotion in the regiment, which his father complied with and paid for the same much more than £200. William remained fully possessed thereof for several years, during which time the regiment embarked for the East Indies during the late war, upon which occasion he was under a necessity of being supplied with divers necessaries in the military way and for considerable sums of money, stores and other commodities, all which Robert supplied him with.

Afterwards Margaret Fitzhugh died, leaving her husband Robert living, who, being greatly advanced in years and weak in body, had retired to Guildford in the county of Surrey. And he continuing to live there and being under great infirmity of body and very much impaired in his understanding, Anne, who was then married and living at Castleford and had several children and a family to take care of, nevertheless being solicitous for the welfare of her father, left her family in Yorkshire and took a journey to visit her father and stayed with him for some considerable time. William, being returned from the East Indies and having quitted his commission, came there also to visit his father.

During Anne's continuance with her father, he at different times, when he was most capable of considering his temporal affairs, and particularly some short time before his death, frequently declared he had fully advanced his son in the world and that he did not intend to make any will and was desirous to give some particular goods to Anne in his lifetime. Then [he] gave her her uncle Warner's, her grandfather Garbrand's, her uncle William Fitzhugh's and her [late] brother Robert's pictures and a cabinet of curious workship and a valuable piece of painting of flowers and some family linen.

One of Anne's children being sick and not likely to live, she was sent for home in Yorkshire and, being under a necessity to return immediately, was obliged to leave the goods and linen in the house where her father then lodged, and desired her brother to take care of them, which he promised to do.

[However, no sooner had Anne left her father alone with her brother than he], being desirous of making his last will, did in or about February 1754 order William to draw up a draft of such a will and did give him instructions for that purpose. He was [William declared] at that time of a sound memory and understanding and not in any manner disordered in his mind, though he then was weak of body ...

And the will bequeathed everything to William and William's son, leaving nothing to Anne. Hence the suit.

Attached to William's Answer was another item of considerable interest, an inventory of his father's household goods.

All that came from one document. And almost all of it of a kind unobtainable from any other source.

My second example has been chosen to show what intimate family detail can be obtained from some equity suits. It is extracted from a case heard in the Court of Star Chamber (STAC.8/108/1) in 1609 and is only one of the many family scenes described in it. The following is the situation that led up to it: in January 1608/9 Robert Fitzhugh, aged 82 and sometimes wandering in his mind, was lying in bed slowly dying. Having three daughters but no sons, he had willed part of his land, being 'the ancient inheritance of the Fitzhughs', to his Fitzhugh nephews (my ancestor among them). This caused a family row in which his wife's niece tore up his will, and then one of his sons-in-law, William Astry, an unscrupulous lawyer, prepared to trick him into sealing a document that would preclude any claim by the nephews for what they had been promised. The scene is late evening in Robert's bedchamber on the ground floor of Paslow's Manor House, Wavendon, Buckinghamshire. The evidence of what happened is contained in depositions by several people present in the room; so the following version, drawn from them all, is the one I wrote for my family history. Everything it describes, every movement, every gesture, every spoken word, is contained in their evidence.

Elizabeth [Robert Fitzhugh's wife, aged about 80], William Astry, Elizabeth Rookes [the niece who tore up the will] and her brother Francis all assembled in Robert's room. Anne Cranwell [a daughter loyal to her father] was already there but she was fast asleep in a chair, 'hanging down her head'. Had her mother slipped some drowsy syrup into her ale, or was it just because she had been up all the night before watching over her father? At any rate, her sleepiness was remarkably convenient, and all their talk did not wake her. Old Robert was in one of his rational spells; and when a night visitor called at the house and was heard speaking to someone in the hall, he remarked: 'There's Wells!'

'It is indeed,' said George Wells, coming into the room. Robert asked what he was doing there at that time of night, to which he replied: 'I came to see how you do.' [That was a lie. He had come by arrangement with Astry as an additional witness of what was about to happen.]

'Not well,' replied the old man, and asked if he had been to bed. Wells said 'No', and Robert remarked: 'It is time for good husbands to be abed now.' Whereupon Wells asked what time of night he thought it was. Robert said: 'About ten or eleven of the clock,' and Wells said it was well guessed.

With Robert so much in his right mind and Wells now present, Astry spoke: 'Mother [in-law], if you please we will move my father about my sister [in-law] Saunders's children.'

She replied: 'Do, if you think good.' So Astry turned to Robert and said: 'Sir, my mother hath a suit to you.'

'What is that?'

Astry produced a document: 'Sir, my mother and I would entreat you to seal this writing.' [We will skip his description of it.]

When Astry had finished speaking, Robert said: 'I hear your mother say nothing.'

Elizabeth, who was sitting near the foot of the bed, rose out of her chair and came and stood beside him. Laying her hand on the coverlet, she said: 'Yes, good Master Robert, grant me this suit. I will trouble you with nothing more. It will never be the worse for Robin Saunders [their grandson], and it will do the younger children good.'

Robert took his wife by the hand and held it a good while. 'Nay, if you request it, you should have it an it were a greater matter.'

Then Astry read out what he had written. . . . Halfway through the reading, a servant, John Heath, came into the room. Aware of the family situation, he took in what was happening and noticed Anne Cranwell asleep in her chair. He moved to wake her, but his mistress and George Wells stood between them.

. . . In fumbling with his signet, the old man accidentally knocked it off the bed with the sleeve of his doublet. So Astry helped him and he sealed the deed. It was then folded up, and he delivered it to his wife, holding her hand a good while as he did so.

What other type of record can bring people long dead so intimately alive?

I have recovered equally detailed scenes and conversations from court cases of the reign of Henry VIII; and the Exchequer case mentioned above cast fascinating light for me on the trade practices, services to customers and competitive nature of the malting business in the town of Bedford in the first half of the seventeenth century.

It is convenient to mention here certain other law courts of which the records of proceedings and evidence survive in writing. These are the ecclesiastical courts of bishops and archdeacons administering canon law. The offences dealt with ranged from heresy, through adultery, fornication, slander, perjury, maladministration of wills, non-attendance at church, misbehaviour in church or churchyard, and failure to pay parish dues. Penalties could include excommunication but were usually penitential admissions of guilt either in private or before the congregation in church. In cases where the offence being tried had come to light at a

Cases of adultery and fornication were among those most frequently brought before archdeaconry courts, but ABOVE Thomas Bragge was suing Joan Crosse for slandering him. A witness for the prosecution had heard her say 'in a very angry and malicious manner' that Thomas had been 'taken in bed with one Alner's wife' and 'his breeches were found in a tub of feathers'. BELOW A case of assault and stabbing which came before the Peculiar (ecclesiastical) Court in 1607, because it took place in a churchyard.

A note of theire Names that have not recevid
at Easter this yere 1608

Roger loopols wife & his mayde
Robert Haytor and his wife                    Joane paynter
peter Donnyten & his wife                     Alice paynter
Richard Tennis & his wife
Thomas Jeary and his wife
Agnes the wife william Tennis
John pike and his wife
Xpofer Silver and alice his wife
Xpofer Lyne and his wife
John Wilder and marye his wife
John Webbe the Tayler & Alice his wife
William Tennis the mother and anne his wife
Alice the wife of Symond Forard
Bastian Jacobbe
Anne Russell
Alice Bisshopp the wife of John Bisshopp of lige
widow roenesse

They that be yet    Thomas Hope
to recevinge for    william Badcocke
Easter last 1608    olde John Boles
                    Pasque John Bissels wife
                    william Tennis
                    Henry Haward at the mills
                    Symon warmyngton
                    mr Barker and his wife
                    William Bundon servant to Thomas Bragge
                    Thomas moere and his wife
                    William painter
                    Alexander roules
                    James Dale Jud
                    the warmyngton widow
                    Alice the wife of Henry ansell
                    william mathew & his wife
                    Symon mathew & his wife
                    Richard pope servant to nicholas vonder
                    John Tyler the yonger
                    Roger loope

previous visitation of the bishop or archdeacon, the accusation against the defendant was brought by the Office of the Judge and the proceedings were brief; but when the charge was brought by one private person against another, they were more formal, and the documents of the plaintiff's Libel of Articles, the defendant's Responsions, the witnesses' Attestations and the Interrogatories corresponded, under their different names, to the records mentioned above of the equity courts. Though the proceedings are recorded in Latin, the documents of most interest to the family historian, the Attestations, are in English; and the witnesses themselves are identified by name, condition, occupation, age and length of abode in parish concerned.

In my experience, few of the proceedings of these ecclesiastical courts have been indexed, but the surviving records, some of them from the fifteenth century, are in the care of the diocesan registries, most of which are now incorporated in the appropriate county record offices.

The records of these equity and ecclesiastical courts offer the family history researcher some of the richest finds he is ever likely to make. For one thing, an accusation and rebuttal are the very stuff of drama, and, on top of that, the personal unsophisticated character of the average witness's evidence tends to provide intimate homely detail almost entirely absent from most source material.

*A list of non-attenders at church for 1608. Recusants, probably all Catholics, are indicated. Continued non-attendance at church would have been brought to the attention of the ecclesiastical court.*

The late nineteenth-century bookplate of Charles Elvin, from his 'Dictionary of Heraldry' republished by Heraldry Today , London . On a small escutcheon of pretence at the centre of the shield are the arms of Elvin's wife who, having no brothers, was an heraldic heiress. Her arms, and those of her husband, are transmitted to their descendants as quarterings. Arms may be identified using reference books such as 'Papworth's Ordinary', which list blazons (heraldic descriptions) of shields alphabetically by the charges they contain. On the helmet (indicative of rank of esquire) is a wreath of twisted silk to which are attached the mantling and crest. Crests can be identified from works such as 'Fairbairn's Book of Crests'; mottoes are notoriously unreliable because they can be changed at will, but are useful as starting points. These are listed in Elvin's own 'Handbook of Mottoes'.

128

# 12

# The ancestor as armiger

In 1887 a volume was published entitled *How to Write the History of a Family* by W.P.W. Phillimore. The author began by listing the various aspects of his subject, including 'heraldry, without some reference to which few family histories can be written'. Could Mr Phillimore return to the genealogical scene he would surely be taken aback by the current widespread interest in ancestry research, the crowds at the General Register Office, the societies and adult education courses all over the country, and the torrent of successors to his book, and all of them making little or no reference to heraldry. However, to those families who are concerned with it, heraldry is not only a valuable aid to genealogical research but an aspect of their own history itself deserving of research.

Our surnames are the ancient family distinguishing mark we all inherit, and which makes genealogical research possible, but as any one surname is more than likely to be shared by families of separate origins, it can also constitute one of genealogy's most difficult problems. However, for armigers, the fact that each coat of arms has been deliberately designed to be unique provides researchers with a valuable means of family identification. What an invaluable aid to genealogy it would have been if the heralds of the College of Arms on their sixteenth- and seventeenth-century rounds of visitation had done the unthinkable thing and granted arms to every single family in the land.

An inherited right to coat armour is an indication of male-line descent from the original grantee, thus distinguishing all legitimate users as members of the same family. Any assumption and use of a family's arms by a person of the same surname but different origin is therefore a falsification, deliberate or otherwise, of his genealogical descent. It is therefore surprising and sad to see any journal of ancestry research accepting advertisements from firms peddling 'arms for your name'.

Yet how many people using a coat of arms in good faith can really be sure that they are entitled to do so by force of a grant to a male-line ancestor? All they usually know is that the arms were borne by their father and grandfather, who would never have stooped to do so illegitimately;

but how do they know that their great-great-grandfather or someone back along their line was not confused by an early armorial bucket-shop merchant, or did not just invent the arms for himself? An armigerous family historian should not let the descent of his arms remain unresearched. Apart from confirming, or otherwise, his right to bear them, the investigation can throw interesting light on areas of his family's past. My father's experiences, followed by my own, bear this out.

*The Arms* When my father started his genealogical researches, he knew our FitzHugh descent as far back as an ancestor born (as he found out later) in London in 1684. But the arms that our family had long been using (*ermine on a chief gules three martlets or*) were those that had been confirmed to a Fitzhugh family of Wilden in Bedfordshire and Wavendon in Buckinghamshire at the Herald's Visitations of those counties back in 1566. At that date they were already quartered with another coat of doubtful attribution. But, for all my father then knew, the gap between our ancestor in London in 1684 and the Bedfordshire armigers of 1566 might not be biologically bridgeable.

That our family's claim to those arms was of long standing was evidenced by several old heraldic fob signets that had been passed to my father. Among them, one showed the 1566 arms impaling those of Hamilton, a heraldic record of my great-great-grandfather's marriage in 1792. And my father's old aunt had a document sealed in 1765 by our ancestor of a generation earlier, displaying the same arms impaling those of Palmentier. Also a collateral branch of our family, descended from a brother born in 1728, had long been using the same arms.

It took some years for my father and his brother-in-law to close the genealogical gap between our ancestor of 1684 and the Bedfordshire family of a century earlier, but they succeeded and, as I mentioned earlier, submitted the documentation of their research to the College of Arms. It was approved by Clarenceux King of Arms, and a formal Confirmation of the martlets and ermine tails was granted in 1930.

All that Clarenceux could say about the arms quartered on the 1566 Fitzhugh shield (*argent, three chevrons sable, each charged with a bezant*) was that they were probably those of either Malabassel or Colville. The uncertainty was owing to the fact that they harked back to the period preceding the foundation of the College. This caused me to do some research into the relative probabilities of a marriage with either of those families. All my searches failed to find any Malabassels within mating distance of the family's ancestral home, the manor of Beggary in the parish of Eaton Socon. On the other hand, I found that a family called Colville had held the adjacent manor of Eaton for one generation in the later fourteenth century. This closest of all possible proximities is still nowhere near proof, but it did make the Colville alternative much the better bet.

My father's submission to the College of Arms of a claim to descent from the sixteenth-century William Fitzhugh of Bedfordshire was not the first that the heralds had received. In 1692, a cousin of my ancestor of that period applied to the College for a confirmation of the 1566 arms and submitted his family tree. His petition was turned down, 'there being no proof in the Books of the Office that his Great Grandfather, John Fitzhugh of Barford in the County of Bedford was the fourth son of William Fitzhugh of Wilden in the said county . . . it will need some better authority before the Arms can be allowed and the Pedigree relied on'. However, that clearly unsuccessful attempt has been of interest to us because Clarenceux· sent my father a copy of the family tree that accompanied it, from which he gleaned useful information about the petitioner's contemporaries.

Another attempt was made in 1885 by a member of a collateral branch of our family. Again the College did not confirm the original arms, but, perhaps taking into consideration the family's long belief in their right to them, accepted them as a basis for a new grant to the petitioner with the addition of certain heraldic 'differences', a fourth martlet in chief and sable flaunches to the ermine field.

*The Crest* The Visitation of 1566 confirmed the arms alone. There was no mention of the crest (*a martlet proper*) that we had always displayed either with it or by itself. A formal Grant of Arms includes a crest to go on the helm, but the sixteenth-century visitations awarded Confirmations to approved families of armorial bearings they had adopted themselves in the days before the College's authority was established. In those days only a minority of families, mainly those of at least knightly status, felt any need of a crest, and the Fitzhughs were not among them. My father would have liked to repair the omission by applying for a grant, but the College's examination of our descent had proved quite expensive enough, so he left it at that. He allowed our existing martlets to perch on undisturbed, but a new signet ring for the son and heir (me) had to accommodate only what was authentic, namely the arms, which were really too large for convenient compression into such a small space.

Eventually, in 1954, I myself approached the College about the possibility of acquiring a crest. Rouge Croix's reply, though discouraging to my intention, was interesting:

> The absence of a Crest in a Coat of Arms is something of a
> distinction, as it indicates that the Arms are ancient. I think I am

right in saying that we have no example of a formal Grant of Arms in which the Crest is omitted, and almost certainly not within the last three hundred years. I think it would therefore be a pity to rob your Arms of their distinction by petitioning the Earl Marshal for the Grant of a Crest.

He suggested that I petition for a badge instead, but I considered a badge an untidy extra, so I dropped the whole idea. Doing nothing solved problems. I could not make up my mind about what crest (or badge) to choose: a fully rigged East Indiaman; a sprig of tea plant; a sea otter? Most of all, I would have liked to make our *martlet proper* really proper, but I had heard that any crest once used illegitimately was never given respectability by a later grant. The grant of 1885 to our collateral branch did include a martlet in the crest, but *erminois* instead of *proper*, and perched on a *quatrefoil sable*.

*The Motto* This item of the heraldic Achievement (the term for a complete heraldic display including, for commoners, arms, crest, motto, helm, torse and mantling) is particularly liable to have a history of its own worth looking into. The aphorism or maxim, usually either sententious (*Persevere*), pious (*Deo non fortuna*), defiant (*Sans reculer jamais*), or punning (*Quisque faber fortunae suae*, of the Faber family), need not necessarily descend through the generations as originally chosen. Any change is therefore likely to reflect some strongly held opinion in the ancestor who made it, and thereby shed light on his character.

Our Fitzhugh motto, *In Moderation placing all my glory*, is a quotation from Alexander Pope's *Satires and Epistles of Horace Imitated*, Book II, Satire I. That work was first published in 1733, which supplies the earliest possible date for the motto's adoption. However, at that time the early death of the father of our family in 1730 had left three boys who all parted company while still under age, leaving England for Syria, Turkey and China respectively. And yet the motto continued to be used by the descendants of two of the brothers (the third did not marry), which argues for agreement between them. If so, this must have come about at some time after they first met again back in England in 1768, two centuries after the original confirmation of the arms.

The choice they made was decidedly unusual. Because heraldic mottoes make their appearance inscribed on a short strip of vellum (called a scroll) depicted beneath the shield — or beneath the crest when used alone — their one necessary common factor is brevity, often carried to the point of obscurity. Also, at that period, the most popular language for mottoes was Latin; but the Fitzhughs picked one that was both exceptionally long and in English; and that in spite of the fact that another quotation, equally well known at that time, advocated moderation both pithily and in Latin, namely the Horatian tag: *Modus in rebus* ('Measure in all things'). This makes me suspect that the brothers' choice expressed a regard not for moderation as a virtue in general, but specifically in the context of Pope's poem, and that was:

> In moderation placing all my glory,
> While Tories call me Whig and Whigs a Tory.

The fact that their sister was the wife of John Purling, a Member of Parliament who sided in the House of Commons sometimes with Prime Minister Pitt the Elder, and sometimes against him, serves further to associate the brothers with a political outlook and one of a centrist character.

In the 1885 grant to our collateral branch, the motto was sensibly shortened to *Moderation is my glory.*

## Ancestors' use and misuse of their arms

Identification of the person to whom your arms were granted can be obtained from the College of Arms, which institution may also have in their files a family tree submitted to them by the grantee. But for the actual use of the arms since the time of the grant, the best sources of information are the wills made and sealed by past members of the family. Such documents enabled me to carry the consistent use of the arms in my branch of the family back to 1713, when again they were found impaling the arms of the current ancestress's family (Pyne of Curry Malet). My ancestor of the generation before that had sealed his will with the illegitimate martlet, the earliest evidence of its use. Then a cousin of mine found a seal of the arms, including the quartering and correctly omitting the crest, made by his ancestor (my ancestor's first cousin) in 1648. This is our earliest evidence of their use since 1566. To find seals on wills, one needs to consult the original documents, not the register copies made by the probate court and routinely produced for present-day examination. The originals are usually equally available at county record offices, but those proved in the Prerogative Court of Canterbury and available at the Public Record Office, Chancery Lane, need to be applied for a week in advance as they have to be brought in from outside London.

An example of the genealogical confusion that using another family's coat of arms is bound to cause occurred in my family when my great-great-aunt Emily, in 1840, heard that there were Fitzhughs living in Virginia, USA. She wrote to her friend Fanny Kemble, living then in Philadelphia, asking her to find out that family's armorial bearings as she was interested to discover whether they might be distant relations. This enquiry resulted in the arrival of a long letter from Boscobel, Stafford County, Virginia. It was signed by William Henry Fitz-hugh junior, and gave a generation-by-generation account of his descent from a William Fitzhugh of Bedford, England, who had emigrated to Virginia in the 1670s, and with it he enclosed an engraving of the arms of a medieval baronial family, the Lords Fitzhugh of Ravensworth Castle in Yorkshire, which had no connection with ours and had in fact become extinct in 1512. He wrote:

> I regret very much, Madam, that I have not the coat of arms delineated with the colours and a neat representation to send you. But, as you doubtless know, under a government like ours the science of heraldry meets with but little encouragement since all the insignia of aristocratic birth and hereditary gentility are most obnoxious to [the] vulgar and ignorant who constitute a majority of our population. This will account for my not having had my attention particularly attracted to the minutiae of the Fitz-hugh coat armour ... The representation sent you is such as my grandfather, Thomas Fitz-hugh, of this house, had painted on his chariot, made in London and imported to this country half a century ago.

As no further letters from William Henry Fitzhugh are among our sparse family papers, it would appear that the seeming lack of relationship, indicated by the different arms, caused the correspondence to lapse. This is a great pity, because the Virginians' notion of their arms was quite incorrect. Their line and Emily's were collateral branches of the same family; and we know now who was originally responsible for the confusion.

The seventeenth-century emigrant to America was the son of Henry Fitzhugh, Mayor of Bedford in 1648, whose surviving seal, already mentioned, shows that he was under no misapprehension as to his ancestry. It was after Henry's death that his younger son William crossed the Atlantic and became a highly prosperous tobacco planter in Virginia. His *Letter Book* (now published as 'William Fitzhugh and his Chesapeake World', edited by Richard B Davis) shows that in 1686 his brother and sister-in-law in London sent him a parcel of presents. One of these was a signet engraved with the family arms; but when William's thank-you letter arrived, it was not at all what they were expecting. He wrote (my italics, of course):

> I heartily thank you for your intended, and your lady's real, presents to my wife, son and daughter, and that steel seal to myself.

Had *she* writ it had been my coat of arms, I should have allowed the mistake, not esteeming her conversant in heraldry or skilful in coats of arms; and for *your* writing it to be so, I must interpret it either to credulity or mistake ...

Far away from England and out of touch with his family, William evidently dreamed of an aristocratic descent from the Lords Fitzhugh of Ravensworth. Having spurned his brother's signet, he had his silver engraved with the baronial family's arms; and his sons and further descendants followed trustingly in his misguided footsteps. It was not until the 1930s, after my father had had an article on our family published in the *Virginia Magazine of History and Biography*, that our American cousins learnt the truth about their lesser gentry origins. It came as quite a shock. Mr Charles C. Carroll, father-in-law of Howard Steptoe Fitzhugh II, wrote to my father:

> The traditional descent of the Virginia Fitzhughs from the Barons of Bardolph [sic], Lords of Ravensworth, has been so generally accepted, and the names 'Eagles' Nest', 'Bedford', 'Marmion', 'Bel Aire', 'Boscobel' so interwoven with American colonial history and genealogy that a call for immediate and unconditional surrender in the claims is naturally somewhat bewildering.

Actually, of course, 'Marmion' was the only one of those estate names that implied a connection with the Yorkshire family, and 'Bedford' positively contradicted it. Today, fifty years later, the American branches seem all aware of their true descent, but, understandably enough, their old silver still retains the imprint of their ancestor's error.

A description of the social role of coat armour, as seen in the reign of Henry VIII, the period when its use was changing from battlefield display to civil status symbol, was written by Sir Thomas Wriothesley, Garter King of Arms, in a grant of 1510 (quoted in *English Historical Documents*, Vol.5, 1485-1558):

> Equity wills and reason ordains that men of virtue of noble spirit should be rewarded for their merits and good renown, and not only their own persons in this brief and transitory mortal life, but, after them, those who should issue and be procreated of their bodies may be renowned in all places perpetually with others by certain signs and tokens of honour and nobility, to wit, with blazon, helm and crest; so that by their example others will be induced to use their days in feats and works of arms, to acquire the renown of ancient nobility in their line and posterity.

This is 'Ercles' vein, and a fitting end to this chapter.

*Setting off to war provoked countless formal informative and often touching photographs, as here, when Harold Pitman was photographed with his parents before leaving for the Front in 1915.*

136

# 13

# The ancestor as Englishman

Our ancestors were influenced in their careers by subterranean shifts in social, economic and political forces of which — in those days before Current Affairs Programmes — most of them will not have had the slightest inkling. Commercial and political trends, the long-term effects of technological inventions, decisive battles, sectarian intolerance, enclosure of fields, humanitarian reforms, bad harvests, Corn Laws and innumerable other forces overrode or undermined for better or worse the aims and efforts of individual Englishmen. In the historian's eyes this does not reduce them to insignificance. On the contrary, when their personal experiences are seen as part of the intricate pattern of epic events, they grow in our interest and respect. The historian therefore needs to make himself aware of the national background to each past generation of his family, and to assess how far their seemingly free activities, when closely examined, were reactions to the historical tides of their time.

The fact, however, that the historian has made himself aware of historical changes in process at any given period is not enough to warrant a bare assumption of their influence on his family. Some actual evidence must be found. At present, however, there is little danger of historical trends being given undue credit in family histories. Too many ancestral narratives treat national events as no more than easily recognisable tags with which to date family incidents. The battle of Trafalgar or the Fire of London, regardless of relevance, gets dragged in to indicate an ancestor's period. One recent history, which actually achieved short-listing in a competition, supplied six generations with their historical context solely by the phrase: 'Lived in the reign of ...', plus, for three of them, the experience of losing eleven days of life through the 1752 change in the calendar. To treat Britain's past, the ancestors' living background, as no more than a parcel of dates is to betray a complete neglect of the preparation needed for writing history. For the serious family chronicler, there is no escaping the need to study the historical background and consider the light it may cast on the family's activities and condition.

The fitting of members of our family into their wider context is often made easy for us by reason of the fact that many of our pieces of family

| Name | C. | P. | K. | M. |
|---|---|---|---|---|
| Borne, John, gentleman, Albany-place, Cowick-street ... | | 1 | | |
| Borne, Henry, gardener, Sanford-street | | | 1 | 1 |
| Boston, F., butcher, Kenton & New Bridge-st, St. Edmunds | 1 | 1 | | |
| Boulter, James, cellarman, Brook Green | | | 1 | 1 |
| Boundy, Samuel, accountant, Magdalen-street ... | 1 | 1 | | |
| Boundy, John, joiner, Waterloo-place | 1 | 1 | | |
| Boundy, George L, clerk, Friars | 1 | 1 | | |
| Boutcher, William, painter, Paris-street | | | 1 | 1 |
| Bovey, Robert, gentleman, Friars Walk | | | 1 | 1 |
| Bowcher, Edward, gentleman, 26, Dix's Fields ... | | | 1 | 1 |
| Bowcher, William, tailor, Parr-street ... | 1 | 1 | | |
| Bowden, George, Cottage-court | | | 1 | 1 |
| Bowden, George, Dymond's-court | | | 1 | 1 |
| Bowden, Thomas, sawyer, Limekiln-lane | 1 | 1 | | |
| Bowden, John, Polsloe Villa, Heavitree | | | — | |
| Bowden, John, bricklayer, Alma-cottage | | | 1 | 1 |
| Bowden, William, bricklayer, Summerland-row | 1 | 1 | | |
| Bowden, John P., plumber, Parr-street | 1 | 1 | | |
| Bowden, John, sawyer, Commercial-road | | | 1 | |
| Bowden, Charles, carpenter, 3, Chapple-buildings | | | 1 | 1 |
| Bowden, W., painter, 8, Spring-tr., York-road, Lambeth | 1 | 1 | | |
| Bowden, William, stone mason, 52, Bartholomew-street... | 1 | 1 | | |
| Bowden, Edward, tailor, Longbrook-terrace | | | 1 | 1 |
| Bowden, Edwin, independent minister, Heavitree | 1 | 1 | | |
| Bowden, William, milkman, St. David's-hill | | | 1 | 1 |
| Bowden, Robt. H. R., yeoman, Woodbury Salterton (fr.) | | | 1 | 1 |
| Bowden, Wm. sawyer, Brunswick-place | 1 | 1 | | |
| Bowden, John, labourer, Lion's Holt ... | | | 1 | 1 |
| Bowden, Wm., sawyer, Summerland street | 1 | 1 | | |
| Bowden, Thomas, junr., sawyer, Townsend-court | 1 | 1 | | |
| Bowden, Thomas, sawyer, Townsend-court | 1 | 1 | | |
| Bowden, Henry, accountant, Melbourne-place | | | 1 | 1 |
| Bowden, John, ironmonger, Magdalen-street | | | 1 | 1 |
| Bowden, William John, 23, Okehampton-street... | | | — | |
| Bowden, David, Elm Grove-road | | | — | |
| Bowden, James, Woodbine-place | | | | |
| Bowden, John, Waterbeer-street | 1 | 1 | | |
| Bowden, Henry, North-street... | | | 1 | 1 |
| Bowdidge, George, West-street | | | 1 | 1 |
| Bowers, Henry, carman, Paul-street | 1 | 1 | | |
| Bowers, George, Edmund-square | 1 | 1 | | |
| Bowring, Henry, tailor, Parr street | 1 | 1 | | |
| Bowring, Sir John, Knight, 3, Claremont Grove | 1 | 1 | | |
| Bowring, John Charles, Larkbeare, St. Leonards | 1 | 1 | | |
| Box, Rev. H. A., Parker's Well House ... | | | — | |
| Boyce, John, gentleman, Union-terrace | 1 | 1 | | |
| Boyce, James, labourer, Black-boy-road | | | 1 | 1 |
| Boyce, Joseph, carpenter, Par-street... | | | 1 | 1 |
| Boyd, the Rev. Archibald, clergyman, the Deanery | | | 1 | 1 |
| Brackenberry, James, Silver-terrace, Heavitree... | | | 1 | 1 |
| Bradbeer, Henry, brushmaker, Friars-walk | 1 | 1 | | |
| Bradbeer, Thomas, North-place | | 1 | | 1 |
| Bradbeer, George, carpenter, Olave's-square | 1 | 1 | | |
| Bradbeer, William Robert, brushmaker, Exe Bridge | 1 | 1 | | |
| Bradbeer, Robert, brushmaker, Paragon-place | 1 | 1 | | |
| Bradbeer, Joseph, brushmaker, St. Sidwell-street | 1 | 1 | | |
| Braddon, John, Currier, Magdalen-street | 1 | 1 | | |
| Braddon, Benjamin, boot closer, King William-terrace ... | 1 | 1 | | |
| Bradford, Thomas, reporter, Parr-street | | | 1 | 1 |
| Bradford, Robt., gardener, Albert-street | 1 | 1 | | |
| Bradford, James, shopkeeper, Paris-street | | | 1 | 1 |
| Bradford, George, joiner, East Wonford | | | 1 | |
| Bradford, James, joiner, Summerland-street | | | 1 | 1 |
| Bradford, William, shoe maker, Pancras lane | | | 1 | 1 |
| Bradford, George, Prospect-place, Rack-street ... | 1 | 1 | | |
| Bradley, William Henry, reporter, Salem-place | 1 | 1 | | |
| Bradley, John, painter, 154, Fore-street | 1 | 1 | | |
| Bradley, William, decorator, 159, Fore-street | 1 | 1 | | |
| Bradley, William Henry, draper, North-street ... | 1 | 1 | | |
| Bradley, Matthew, gent, 1, Richmond-terrace, St. Leonard | | | 1 | 1 |
| Bragg, George, builder, Portland-place | | | 1 | |
| Brailey, Charles, chemist, Heavitree ... | 1 | 1 · | | |

*The Exeter Parliamentary Election, 1868. A poll book is a first clue to an ancestor's political opinions. Here the four letters at the head of the right-hand columns are the initials of the parliamentary candidates (Coleridge, Bowring, Karslake, Mills), and the placing of the figures beneath them indicates for which ones the ancestor voted.*

evidence were documented in the first place only because of their national causation. One example of this is the parliamentary vote to which all owners of freeholds rated at 40 shillings per annum were entitled, and the right everyone had, from 1696 till 1868, to ascertain how every vote had been cast. This accessibility was intended to prevent falsification of the poll by corrupt returning officers. Its importance to us now is that it gave rise to the publication of post-election Poll Books, on a county basis, listing the electors and showing for which candidates they had voted. These put us in the way of discovering our ancestors' political opinions.

After the general election of 1780, the Poll Book for Hampshire showed that the two candidates my ancestor had voted for were John Fuller (a sitting member), and Hans Sloane (a newcomer), and that they both got in at the expense of John Fleming (the other sitting member). *The History of Parliament, House of Commons, 1764-1789*, Vol.II, reveals that Fuller and Sloane were strong supporters of the policies of Prime Minister Lord North, whereas Fleming had lately turned against him in the House of Commons. Lord North is, of course, now best remembered for his efforts to coerce our American colonists.

Two generations later, in the election of 1837, another ancestor's political opinions were revealed by the speeches of candidates being printed in the East Sussex Poll Book, as was the frequent though not invariable practice. Candidate George Darby declared:

> I believe it to be the sacred duty of every man to use his utmost energies to defend the Protestant constitution against the attacks of those Roman Catholic agitators who obtained power under the promise of peace ... I am persuaded of the necessity of adequate protection to British capital and labour, whether employed in agriculture or manufactures, and am most decidedly opposed to Free Trade in either the one or the other.

And those were the Revd William FitzHugh's sentiments, too.

A third source of information as to the candidates' political opinions is the local newspaper for the weeks leading up to the election. An ancestor becomes much more interesting when we know how he personally felt about the way the country was being run. But that applies only if you paint in enough of the current political situation to give his opinions significance.

Parliamentary elections are only one simple example of the links to be discovered between the individual and our national history. There are many others. The Reformation and redistribution of monastery lands under Henry VIII, the Puritan Revolution of the early seventeenth century, the Civil War and Restoration, all gave rise to documentary opportunities for the family historian to show his characters in the grip of national events and trends. Then in the eighteenth century came the New Agriculture, the expansion of world trade, the beginnings of the Industrial Revolution and the British Empire, any one of which is likely to have affected our forebears' lives and given rise directly or indirectly to written evidence. The following quoted records, one or two per century, picked out in chronological order from many others, supply successive instances of links between schoolbook history and that of my own particular family.

First the fourteenth century and the Hundred Years War. When John Fitzhugh of Beggary and the Vill of Wyboston was murdered in 1358, his killer fled and was outlawed, but the hand of justice was diverted by a pardon offered by King Edward III to criminals giving satisfactory military service in his campaign to capture Rheims from the French king. Though the expedition was a failure, the king kept his word, and three years later the following writ, shown in *Calendar of Patent Rolls*, Vol.XI, was issued:

> Pardon, for good service in the war of France in the company of Roger de Bello Campo [Beauchamp] to Richard le Stokkere of Beggary . . . for the death of John, son of William son of Richard [Fitzhugh] of Wyboston, and Peter, servant of the said John; also for having entered the close of the said John at Beggary, ravished Elizabeth his wife, stolen a horse worth 16s and a saddle worth 6s 8d and carried away other goods.

That same Hundred Years War caused the Fitzhughs trouble running into the fifteenth century, because the overlord to whom they held their manor was the monastery of St Neot's in Huntingdonshire, which, being ecclesiastically subordinate to the Abbey of Bec in Normandy, was classed as an 'alien priory' and taken into the king's hands every time hostilities with France were resumed.

In the sixteenth century, during the Dissolution of the Monasteries by Henry VIII, I found from *Transactions of the Royal Historical Society*, 4th ser., Vol.16, that in 1538 my ancestor's brother Thomas, who was a judge, was one of three on the bench when the Abbot of Woburn pleaded guilty to having uttered the words:

> The Bishop of Rome's authority is good and lawful within this realm according to the old trade; and that is the true way, and the contrary, of the King's part, but usurpation deceived by flattery and adulation.

And to having aggravated his offence by adding:

> It is a marvellous thing that the King's Grace could not be
> contented with that noble Queen, his very true and undoubted
> wife, Queen Katherine.

The judicial sentence for expressing such treasonable sentiments was
mandatory, and the judges duly pronounced it. The Abbot was
condemned to be hanged, drawn and quartered.

Next, the seventeenth century and the struggle between King and
Parliament. The following extract from the *Journal of the Common Council
of the City of London* for 20th March 1641, showed my ancestor hampered
in his hosiery business by the political troubles leading to the civil war, in
this particular case by parliament's impeachment of the king's chief
adviser, Thomas Wentworth, Earl of Strafford:

> Whereas by order this day made by the Lords Spiritual and
> Temporal in the High Court of Parliament assembled, myself [the
> Lord Mayor], the aldermen and sheriffs of this City are to ... give
> command that several guards be set for the keeping of the
> apprentices and others within the City during the trial of the Earl
> of Strafford, that a concourse come not into Westminster during
> the time of the trial ... These are to ... require you ... that you take
> especial care and give a strict command that on Monday next a
> double watch and ward be constantly kept all that day within your
> Ward from 5 of the clock in the morning until 9 at night ... and so
> to be continued until further order be given in this behalf for the
> suppressing of any tumults that may happen to arise ... And also
> that you cause commandment to be given to every inhabitant
> within your Ward to be very careful to keep their apprentices and
> servants within doors, that they may not wander abroad out of the
> City during the trial aforesaid ...

So William Fitzhugh in the first house on London Bridge had to keep
young Nathaniel Smith indoors for nearly a month until the king's
favourite minister was finally attainted by his enemies. And linked with
that, an appendix to the *6th Report of the Royal Commission on Historical
Manuscripts*, showed that from his house at the Bridge Foot the hosier and
his family must have seen the distinguished prisoner being brought daily
by river from the Tower of London to his trial in Westminster Hall,
because he was taken out of the barge when it reached the Bridge,
conducted across the Bridge Foot within view of the Fitzhughs' front
windows and down again to the river by the Bear Inn steps, just below
their windows at the back.

1. Yorke house.
2. Durham house.
3. New exchainge.
4. Savoy.

5. Somerset house.
6. Arundel house.
7. Essex house.
8. Temple.

9. Baÿnards cast.
10. St Andre in Holb.
11. St Pawls Church.
12. Boo Church.

13. Guild hall
14. St Lorentz Poultney.
15. the Royal exchainge.
16. St Michael.

17. St Petrus.
18. St Duston in the East.
19. Alhallows harking.
20. Cofton house.

*The most traumatic event in the history of the English capital, the Fire of London, 1666. William Fitzhugh would have watched from his home on the south bank of the river as the flames destroyed his property on the north.*

Later that century, when the city of London was destroyed by fire, William's home at the Southwark end of London Bridge lay outside the danger area, but he held a long lease on a property at the corner of Philpot Lane and Fenchurch Street which was destroyed in the holocaust. A little over a year later, evidently after some haggling on William's part (he was at first offered a shorter lease) landlord and leaseholder came to the following agreement, as recorded in the *Journal of the Bridge House Committee*, Vol.2:

> Ordered and agreed that William Fitzhugh, Merchant Taylor, surrender the two old leases yet in being ... of a messuage lately standing at the corner of Philpot Lane in Fenchurch Street and back rooms, etc. destroyed in the late Fire (in both which were 53 years to come at Michaelmas last) and in consideration of his loss thereof and that he rebuild the same according to the late Act, shall and may have a new lease of the premises, cellars and ground, not staked out, for 81 years from Michaelmas last under the accustomed yearly rent of £10 ...

Moving into the eighteenth century, Britain's accession of new colonies in the West Indies after her victories over France and Spain in the Seven Years War led to the following announcement, recorded in *The Annual Register* for 1764:

> March 26. This day His Majesty signed a proclamation for the sale by auction of all His Majesty's lands in the islands of Grenada, the Grenadiines, Dominica, St Vincent and Tobago excepting such lands as shall be necessary for fortifications and other military works, glebes for ministers, allotments for schoolmasters, high roads, woodlands and other public purposes, under the following conditions: That the purchasers pay 20 per cent of the whole purchase money down, 10 per cent in one year, 10 per cent in the second year and 20 per cent every year after till all is paid. That every purchaser shall have one white man or two white women for every 100 acres cleared or pay £20 for every white woman and £40 for every white man wanting. That sixpence per acre shall be paid to the Crown as a quit rent on such lands as shall be cleared . . .

These were the conditions under which my ancestor's brother William, as already mentioned, acquired for the family a sugar plantation in St Vincent in the Windward Islands.

On to the nineteenth century and a date recognisable by all. Among the Society of Genealogists' *Deposited Manuscripts* I found a copy of a letter describing an experience of Mary Lance, née Fitzhugh (my ancestor's sister), and her family in 1815. They were staying in Brussels and had attended the famous ball broken up by news of Napoleon's rapid advance on the city. Mary's daughter, in a letter to her cousin in England, recounted their experience, so similar to that of Amelia Sedley in Thackeray's *Vanity Fair*.

> The following morning (the 17th June) Papa was awaked by the galloping of horses and the cries of 'Fermez les portes!' . . . He got up and saw 100 Prussian Lancers galloping down the street, some with heads bound, others without eyes [sic]. He was convinced the Prussians were retreating and fully expected to see the French follow. However, upon enquiry he learned they were runaways. Soon after, the wounded began to come in, and a most dreadful sight it was. Mrs Erskine (very big with child and whose husband was engaged) spent the day with us and could not be prevailed

OVERLEAF *Part of a letter home from John Lewis of the 95th Regiment, 8th July 1815. An ancestor who can provide a participant's account of what happened during the Battle of Waterloo leaves a treasure indeed for the family historian.* 143

Dear Father Mother brother and Sisters.

I make no doubt but you have heard of the Glourie's News & I suppose you thought I was killed or wounded but yeasterday is the first day we have halted since the begining of the Battle on the 18th of June & my hands are swelled so with walking day and night that I scarce can hold my pen I do not know what the English Newspapers say about the Battle but thank God I am livining & was an Eye witness to the begening of the Battle to the Ending of it but my pen cannot Explain to you nor twenty Shets of paper yould not contain what I could say about it for thank God I had my health & strength more on the Days we was engaged than ever I had in my life so what I am going to tell you is real truth but I think my brother Thomas as he is such a scollar if he was to look at the Newspaper he might see what Officers was killed & wounded of the 95 Regment we have but six companies in the Country & before the Battle we was 550 Strong & this morning we was not 295 so we lost of our Regment 255 Privates two Cournals One Major 15 Officers 11 Sargants & one Buglar my front rank man was Wounded by a part of a shele through the foot & he dropt as we was advancing I covered the next man I saw and had not walked twenty steps before a Musket shot came sideways and took his nose clean off & than I covered another man wich was the third, just after that the man that stood next to me on my left hand had his left arm shot of by a Nine pound Shot just above his Elbow & he turned round & caut hold of me with his right hand & the blood ran all over my trowsers we was advancing so he Dropt Directly after this we was ordered to Extend in front of all & our Large Guns was fireing over our heads & the Enemeys Large Guns & smale arms was fireing at the British lines in our rear & I declare to God with our Gunes & the french Gunes fireing over our heads my pen cannot Explain aney thing like it - it was not 400 Yards from the French lines to our British Lines & we was about 150 yards in front of ours, so we was about 250 yards from the French & sometimes not One

hundred

hundred Yards so I leave you to judge if I haden a —
norrow escape for my life. as I just said we was extended
in front Bonneys Imperil Horse Guards all cloathed in —
Armour made a charge at us we saw them coming & we
all closed in & formed a square just as they come —
within 10 yards of us & they found they could do no good
with us they fired with their Carbines on us & come to
the right about Directly / & at that moment the man on
my right hand was shot through the body & the blood
run out of his Belley & Back like a Pig stuck in the —
thought he drop on his side I spoke to him he just
said Lewis I am don & died Directly / all this time we
kept up a constant fire at the Imperil Guards they reateded
but they often came to the right about & fire / and as
I was loding my rifle one of their shots came & struck —
my rifle not two Inches above my left hand as I was
ramming down the ball with my right hand & broke the
stock & bent the barrel in such a manner that I could
not get the bale down just at this time we extended —
again & my rifle was of no good to me a Nine pound shot
came and cut the serjant of our company right in two he
was not above three file from me so I through down my
rifle and went and took his Rifle as it was not hurt / at —
this time we had lost both our Cournals, Major, and the
two oldest Captains & onely a young Captain to take —
command of us for Cournal Wade he was sent to England
about three weeks before the battle. seeing we had lost
so many men & all our Commanding Officels my hart begun
to fail — & Bonneys Guards than made another Charge on
us but we made them retreat as before & while we war in
square the second time the Duke of Wellington and all
his Staff came up to us in the midst of all the fire &
saw we had lost all our Commanding Officers. he himself gave
the word of Command / the words he said to our Regiment
was this / 95th unfix your sords left face & extend ——
yourselves once more we shale soon have them over the —
other Hill / & then he rode away on our right & how he —
escape being shot God only knows for at this time the —
shots was flying like haill storms / this was about 4 Clock
on the 18th June when Wellington Rode away from our ——
Regment — & then we advanced like Britons but we could
not go five steps without walking over the dead & wounded
& Bonneys Horses of the Imperial Guards that the men
was killed was running loose about in all Directions / if
our Tom had ben little behind in the rare he might catch
Horses enough to had a troop or two like Sir John De La Pool —
Wellington

upon to leave the window; and we remained there to prevent her seeing some of the most dreadful sights. Poor Captain Erskine lost one arm and two fingers of the other hand on the 18th, and his life was despaired of some days by the amazing loss of blood ... His arm literally streamed all the way from Waterloo to Brussels (nine miles)...

A few years later, the Industrial Revolution in Britain took a new step forward with the application of steam power to transport. In 1820 my ancestor took a share in the first steam vessel to ply between Southampton and the Isle of Wight. On 20th July, as reported in the local press:

The long expected steam vessel (*Prince Cobourg*) began to run between Southampton and Cowes as a regular Post Office packet. She performed the voyage to Cowes and back three times in a day, being a distance of nearly 90 miles, part of which was necessarily against the wind and tide. This fine vessel must be a great convenience to passengers, particularly in calms, when [up to the present] only open [rowing] boats may be used.

On to the beginning of the twentieth century, close enough to the present day for oral evidence to throw personal light on what was, at least in my father's eyes, the most exciting technological development of the age. The story of my parents' honeymoon in 1906 was told me by my mother and noted down by me not at all in the systematic manner of today's oral historians. My father had hired a motor car with a chauffeur, so that after the wedding in Edinburgh the pair of them could be wafted by the marvel of modern science through the romantic highland scenery of the Trossachs. The reality turned out to be rather less glamorous. Whenever

June 6, 1906
On the road from Pitlochry to Loch Maree.

they came to a steep section of the road, my parents had to get out of the car, unload their luggage and carry it up the hill, while the driver turned the vehicle round and drove it up backwards in the only gear capable of making the gradient and realising a honeymoon dream somewhat ahead of its time.

The beginning of the twentieth century leads on to World War I, the event that engulfed men of nearly every family. Here, if nowhere else, the family historian will have exciting ancestral experiences to relate. In my family, three brothers were in the army — my father as a chaplain, my uncle Terrick a regular officer, and my uncle Valentine, who came home from America to join up in his county regiment, the Royal Sussex. His battalion, the 8th, were Pioneers, whose duties at the front were the construction, maintenance and repair of trenches, saps, dug-outs, tracks and breastworks and the conversion of captured enemy positions into strong-points for our own troops. The adjutant's war diaries enable me to pick up his battalion's movements from the time it set out from Codford in Wiltshire for France and the Western Front.

These war diaries record the daily experiences of each battalion and its constituent companies. They and the copies, filed with them, of Operation Orders from higher command are preserved at the PRO, Kew, under class WO.95. Studied together they transport the mind of the researcher in to the grim detail of epic events. In June 1916 one Operation Order informed my uncle's battalion, 'The 18th Division is about to take part in a General Offensive'. This was to be the phase of the war now known as the First Battle of the Somme. Further Orders during the next fortnight issued detailed instructions and information, from which the following is a small selection:

> The Infantry assault will be preceded by a 5 days' bombardment by guns of all calibre and mortars. ... Infantry Brigades will arrange for rifle and machine gun fire to be kept up intermittently throughout every night to assist the Artillery in preventing the enemy repairing damaged wire. ... On the first favourable opportunity between U and Y day there will be a simultaneous discharge of gas all along the front line. The Infantry assault will take place on Z day.

> Eight underground saps are nearly completed to within 20 yards of the enemy's front trenches. Mine charges will be laid at the forward ends and exploded just before the assault. ...

> One wireless set will be moved forward with the attacking troops ... Eight birds [pigeons] will be sent daily to Bronfay Farm by

motor cyclist from Etinehem. These birds will be distributed to Infantry Brigades under orders to be issued later ... The attacking Infantry will signal to aeroplanes by means of (1) Flares; (2) Mirrors ...

And two days before Z day, came a warning:

1.   All ranks must be on their guard against the various ruses at which the enemy has shown himself to be adept, especially the use of British words of command, such as 'Retire', etc.
2.   The German machine gun is carried on a sledge, and the Germans sometimes throw a blanket over the gun. This makes the sledge and gun resemble a stretcher.

... the use of 'Retire' as a shouted order must be absolutely forbidden and the troops told that they are to ignore it entirely, no matter from whom they hear it.

The task allotted to my uncle's unit was:

... opening up communications across No Man's Land on the south half of the Division's front ... 'A' Company will be responsible for opening up and policing saps 1 and 2 and will also take over saps 3 and 4. In the event of the pre-arranged saps being so badly damaged as to be beyond repair, the companies concerned will open up other communications, digging fresh trenches altogether if necessary.

On Z day the diary began:

7.30 a.m. The Division attacks ...

On that one day, 1st July 1916, the British Fourth Army lost 56,835 men killed, wounded and missing, more than on any other day in the whole war; and the diary of each battalion recorded its own losses. The offensive continued for months with disappointing gains, and on 29th September the adjutant of the 8th Royal Sussex recorded:

... Casualties today:
Major V.M. FitzHugh wounded;
2/Lt G.A. Cowley wounded slightly, at duty;
No. G/2694 Pte Wickenden, G. (C Company) wounded;
No. G/2117 L/Sgt Stunt, A. (A Company) wounded slightly, at duty.

These battalion casualty lists are one means of ascertaining the company to which a man belonged; so it is unfortunate that many adjutants, while identifying officers by name, gave only daily totals of casualties for other ranks. However, as can be seen from the above extracts, knowledge of a man's battalion is sufficient to enable the family historian to write a graphic chapter on the mind-chilling hardships and dangers endured by one generation of his family's menfolk.

World War I is a climax in our series of ancestral links with national history; but to end the chapter on a happier note I turn back to a late nineteenth-century occasion of celebration in which pretty well every British man and woman, and therefore our ancestors themselves, took part, and about which there is a good chance of description in print. Tuesday the 21st June 1887 and the same date ten years later marked the Golden and Diamond Jubilees of Queen Victoria. On the occasion of the first of these the *Sussex Advertiser* noted that sixty-five bonfires had been erected in the county:

> constructed on the principles laid down by the Lord Lieutenant . . . about 35 ft high. The signal to light will be given by the firing rockets from Ditchling Beacon.

The parish magazine for Streat, Sussex, described how the Jubilee was celebrated in that village:

> The Anniversary of the Queen's Accession was kept as a general holiday. At half past ten there was a Thanksgiving Service in Church, which was attended by nearly every man (and a good many of the women) in the parish. The Anthem 'They set the Royal Crown upon her head' was followed by the Rector's address; and a march was played as voluntary in going out . . . The public dinner followed in a booth erected by the Committee . . . After the loyal toasts had been duly honoured, the company adjourned to the field, where a cricket match for the men and stoolball for the women beguiled the beautiful afternoon. Then came a substantial tea, followed by sports, amongst which the tug of war, sackbag, egg and obstacle races were conspicuous, suitable prizes having been provided for the winners. Last of all came dancing on the green till sundown, when most of the party adjourned to witness the bonfires on the hill.

Continuous evidence of interaction between the private past of our own folk and the public past of our country stirs a lively sense of the family's continuous presence in the drama of history; and we recognize our bygone kin as characters from earlier episodes of the great epic serial in which we ourselves are now appearing.

# 14

# Writing the narrative

I used to tell my students that writing their family history was the last thing they should do. I meant that if they rushed into it, they would then either have to give up their fascinating hobby or continue with their family researches and be for ever issuing revised editions of their history. I must, however, admit that I took my own advice somewhat too literally. Relatives kept asking me: when are you going to give us the family history? And I always replied that I had not yet discovered all there was to be found. I was then under the impression that starting on the narrative would mean stopping the research, which was a pursuit I dearly loved. However, when at last, pressed by enquiries from distant cousins in America, I did sit down and tap out 'Chapter 1', I found the process not at all what I had expected. The weaving of my items of evidence into a continuous story kept posing new questions and giving me fresh ideas; so that I was — and still am — constantly hurrying off again to the Public Record Office or wherever, to find the answers. So the writing stage goes hand in hand with supplementary research, and the two together make progress extremely slow. Several years, twenty-four chapters and 542 quarto pages (1½ spaced) later, I am still at it. Starting from the Middle Ages, I have so far only reached down to 1768, leaving me a long way yet to go. So when tempted to start writing your history, consider the danger of producing a work you may later look back on as premature and immature, but at the same time think how many years ahead it may take to do justice to the centuries behind you.

A word, however, for those who are far from over-hasty and feel, as I once did, that while the recovery of lost events of the family's past is fascinating, the prospect of making a readable book out of them is so intimidating that the start gets constantly put off. My experience now is that once you have your first chapter behind you, you will find that telling the story is the most rewarding stage of the whole ancestral enterprise.

In this chapter, I aim to air the problems that are either peculiar or specially relevant to the actual writing of family history. I encountered them all without any prior expectation of their difficulties, and would have been glad to come across someone like me, prepared to chat in print about coping with them, even if I totally disagreed with him.

When I began my historiography, the first decision I had to make was: what sort of narrative history was I going to write? A choice had to be made and then kept to. The alternatives before me were: writing either as a historian or as a storyteller. As the former, I should be free to make full use of hindsight and to express twentieth-century judgments. As the latter, I must *appear* to know nothing but what was happening at the time. If an ancestor of the early eighteenth century obtained employment with Abraham Darby at Coalbrookdale, a 'historical' historian might well mention that he was getting in on the ground floor of the Industrial Revolution; and if his son was recruited to fight the rebellious colonists in America, the historian might send him off with some warning on the futility of the expedition. Not so the storyteller, though he might drop the reader little clues to let him become aware of the wider aspects of the situation seemingly for himself. My personal preference was for storytelling. I think that was because it would enable me to make use of the constant uncertainty of my characters' future as a device for holding the reader's attention. However, do not let me influence you. Both alternatives are of course equally valid.

Whichever choice you make between those basic approaches, you will now have to make up your mind on a few further alternatives. One way of writing a family history is as detective story, with yourself (the author) as the central character, discovering scraps of evidence, following up clues and testing hypotheses. This can be made exciting, though personally I think it more likely to interest fellow genealogists than the general reader. Also it involves telling the family's story backwards, with effects before causes. However, it copes with one problem by making a virtue of it. It authenticates the historian's statements by giving the discovered documentary evidence priority over the family story it reveals.

At one time it was considered that the function of the narrative historian was to tell what happened. Now it is realised that this is altogether too much to expect. In reality, all he can do is to interpret the evidence he has found. Yet even if his research brings every scrap of surviving documentation to light, the evidence it contains may still be incomplete or inaccurate or both, so that all his skill in interpretation can make his version of events no more than the nearest he can get. This means that no original historical writing has any validity beyond the evidence upon which it is based. Therefore that evidence must be made available to any critical reader. It is only 'popular histories' re-telling events already known to have been thoroughly researched that can afford to dispense with reference to the evidence for its authentication.

## Writing the narrative

Supposing you do not adopt the detective story treatment and decide to tell your ancestral story in conventional chronological order, your next decision will lie between two alternative methods of authenticating it. A family's story is a research trail never trodden before; so every family statement will need to be substantiated. Most of the narrative family histories I have browsed through do this by accompanying each statement with a mention, in the text, of its documentary source. To me, this is like building a house and leaving the scaffolding up. What reader, except a fellow historian, wants the tale of his family cluttered up with constant mentions of historical records about which he neither knows nor cares? Also, this in-text authentication, spotlighting each piece of evidence, tends to induce a first-time historian to treat some of the documentary evidence as ancestral events in themselves. So one often sees a national census mentioned as an item of family history; and yet how many of us remember filling up even our last census form?

Though a source reference for each family statement is essential, it should be supplied in such a way as not to interrupt the flow of attention of the general reader, who is only interested in what happened next. This is customarily achieved by placing in the text small numerals raised above the line, where they catch the eye only of a reader looking for them; and these numerals (known to printers as superior numbers) refer to documentary sources identified elsewhere. This practice will be described in detail a little later.

Actually, I do make certain exceptions to the practice of excluding source details from my historical text. There are one or two occurrences in my family story that seem to lie so outside the current ancestor's normal way of life that I have felt that even the most general of readers is likely to wonder whether it was really he who was involved and not some other man of the same name; and on such occasions I have felt obliged to mention in the text my reason for identifying him.

*What sort of readers are we aiming at?* Mainly the members of our own family and their descendants; and they, as far as historical knowledge goes, will mostly fall in the General Reader class. Presumably our years of research and historical reading will have put us ahead of most of them, but each of us will have some idea of how much background history we can safely afford to take for granted. We do not want to take our readers out of their depth nor to appear naive.

*Language* Family historians are among those rare authors who can settle down to their work with the reasonable expectation that it will be read by generations yet unborn. The thought should be a warning: pick your words carefully. Though you may be keen to produce a popular work — popular, that is, with your living relatives — you must not forget your descendants. Readers a century or two hence may well find the slang and colloquialisms of the late twentieth century quaint or even puzzling. To create a lasting family classic, standard English is the only safe usage. Even that, of course, is changing under our eyes. To mention the Fire of London as a *holocaust*, as I have done, is correct because it was indeed 'a large conflagration' (*Oxford English Dictionary*), but the frequent use of the word to mean 'wholesale slaughter' is supported, though on weaker etymology, by Collins's dictionary. And I have even seen the organising by the Federation of Family History Societies of a party to visit Salt Lake City described, by someone really only surprised at the scale of the operation, as an 'enormity', which means monstrous wickedness (OED). The process of change is always going on. We can but take care, with the aid of several dictionaries, a thesaurus and a little pedantry, to write as correctly as possible and hope we shall continue to be understood by many generations yet.

*Continuity* Most of us are researching the lives of ordinary private people unknown to fame, so, however thoroughly we go about it, we are unlikely to be able to trace their careers steadily month by month or even year by year, and, when we come to writing, we shall find ourselves faced with gaps in our raw material that threaten to reduce a life story to a series of unconnected anecdotes. These gaps must be filled if our readers' attention is to be maintained. The solution often lies in the continuity of a common context. For example, if two incidents separated by a gap of years are both related to an ancestor's occupation, the best way to deal with them may be to introduce them á propos when you are describing that occupation. I myself found no documentary mention of young William Fitzhugh between 1613, when he was apprenticed for nine years to a member of the Merchant Taylors Company, and 1622, when he became free. However, I filled the gap by describing what it meant to be one of those immature, idealistic, unruly London apprentices in the formative years of the Puritan Revolution, mentioning actual instances of their mob behaviour during the period of William's servitude, adding also information about how the household in which he was living was becoming progressively crowded as children were born to the master and his wife; and I led up to the end of William's servitude by mentioning the engagement, some months previously, of a new apprentice to step into his shoes. I do not think I left much room in the reader's mind for any sense of hiatus.

Gaps occurring just before the two vital genealogical events of birth and death can be shortened and a sense of anticipation created by mentioning, in the former case, the pregnancy and, in the latter, the terminal illness, plus, from 1837 onwards, the first summoning of the doctor. The middle genealogical event, marriage, also provides an opportunity for filling in the period leading up to it, but I have commented on that already.

Sometimes a gap can be filled or minimised by supplementary research, looking for something that obviously must have happened during the empty period. On the day after Christmas 1735 an East Indiaman ship was captured by Indian pirates off the Malabar coast and her crew taken into slavery. Her 2nd Mate was the son of Eleanor Cuddon née Fitzhugh, and in the following October, after a gap of ten months, she and the other officers' next-of-kin in England addressed an appeal to the East India Company's directors to do something about getting them freed. For me this raised the question: when and how did she first get to know about the capture? So I searched in the Burney Collection of Newspapers, and in the *Daily Post* for 7th July 1736 (as soon after the capture as, at that distance, could reasonably be expected), I found a report of the disaster bought by a returning East Indiaman.

> Yesterday the purser of the *Beaufort*, Capt. Boulton, arrived at the East India House in Leadenhall Street with the agreeable news of the safe arrival of the said ship off the Isle of Wight from Bengal. She was in company with the *Queen Caroline*, Capt. Wilkie, from Bombay last, whose purser not being come up yet, we must defer particulars of the taking of the *Derby*, Capt. Anselme, a large ship belonging to the East India Company, by Angria, a pirate, near Bombay.

(In today's newspapers, it would of course have been 'FIRST THE BAD NEWS'.)

There followed first a partial retraction by the *Post*, then a confirmation; so my supplementary search produced material that not only shortened the gap but also provided a worried mother with fluctuating periods of hope and fear.

Another threat to the continuity of a reader's attention comes from the opposite direction: items of family information that distract from, instead of carrying on, the narrative flow. You will often come across a mere scrap of ancestral mention, unsatisfying because it raises questions that all your searches fail to answer. At the end of the sixteenth century one member of my family was taken to court for a debt, but there is no record of why the debt was incurred, why it was not repaid or how the case ended, and no sign of any long-term consequence; so in my family history I just left it out. Inclusion of such indeterminate items means turning off the narrative highway into frustrating cul-de-sacs, followed by backing out again on to the main road. I strongly advise against mentioning items of information for no better reason than that you have discovered them. In story telling, too much is as dangerous as too little. A bore is someone who mentions everything.

*Overlapping lives* What makes a family history different from other historical literature is that it consists of a series of interlinked biographies extending over centuries. So the main literary problem lies in the skilful arrangement of many necessarily 'brief lives'. Sometimes they can, or must, be delivered in chunks, a whole life at a time; but more often the narrative involves switching from one character in mid-career to another and back again. This 'Meanwhile back at the ranch' technique often comes in handy for plugging gaps in continuity. In using it, you need to give the impression that you and your reader are being called away to something more interesting. Later you return to the first subject, and nobody worries that you are not resuming from the point where you quitted it.

*Action* A documented mention of an ancestor is usually a record of something just done by or to him. He was apprenticed, or married, or taken to court, or buried, or whatever. The need to take such statements as a starting point tends to induce in the historian a passive state of mind which makes him write of these events as things done. But a reader will be interested in the ancestor actually doing them or having them done to him, and in having the action circumstantially described. For instance, the Merchant Taylors' records say that in 1613 William Fitzhugh *was apprenticed* to Edward Peirce; but, after some background research, it is much more interesting to write something like this:

> Before any member of the Merchant Taylors Company could take a new apprentice, the boy had to be brought before the Master and Wardens in Common Hall assembled for them to question him to make sure he was fully qualified, through being a subject of the King either by birth or naturalisation, of the right family background and under no prior binding. So as soon as those august personages were met, Peirce took William, probably accompanied by his father [from Southwark], into the heart of the City to his interview. Through the narrow streets of half-timbered buildings they made their way to Threadneedle Street and the group of buildings from which it had acquired its name, the headquarters of the Merchant Taylors Company. They entered the great hall where the public functions of the company were held. Its

ancient floor was still of brick and strewn with rushes, but its walls were panelled and hung with tapestries on which were worked scenes from the life of the gild's patron saint, St John the Baptist . . .

*Historical intuition* Except for a survivor from the Edwardian era like myself, this last quarter of the twentieth century is a particularly difficult period from which to transport oneself mentally back into the social modes of thought of our ancestors. Within my lifetime, attitudes and opinions have changed more than in the previous three or four centuries. The past being, as someone has remarked, another country, we must not judge our forefathers or their contemporaries by the social standards of present-day Britain. Certain inhabitants of my childhood world have ceased to exist: sinners, niggers, perverts, bastards, lunatics, drunkards, fallen women and lots of other colourful characters. Likewise, to a great extent, social distinctions between classes, sexes and races. Likewise again, from further back, the transportation of petty thieves, purchase of army commissions, registration of infants as baseborn and many other bygone usages. All those attitudes, distinctions and practices are liable to be encountered on our quest into the past; and the people we meet there will be found regarding them as normal aspects of their social scene. So beware — any naive utterances of righteous indignation from you, an outsider from the future, will simply reveal a lack of historical intuition. Almost the only occasions when it is safe for the family historian to express condemnation of past conduct are infractions of the Ten Commandments, laws more generally respected in those times than they are today. Otherwise it is best to keep your opinions to yourself, leaving readers free to react according to their own individual understandings.

The same applies to expressions of smirking superiority. It is tempting but wrong to be facetious at the expense of physicians and their prescriptions in the days when blood was tapped and alcohol and Daffy's Elixir prescribed for almost every illness. When purser Thomas Fitzhugh was suffering from bloody flux on the unhealthy Hooghly River in 1731, I was careful to describe his symptoms and their treatment as they were seen at the time, by quoting from Surgeon John Moyle's manual, *The Sea Chirurgion*:

It is a lamentable disease, voiding of blood from ulceration and scanners of the guts [caused by] the unnatural choler that gnaws and frets the tender tunicles of the intestines . . . not without tormenting and violent pain.

However, it was treatable:

> The medicines made of rhubarb are known and experienced to be the best, because they not only purge choler but also leave a restrictive quality behind; yet it must be mixed with such ingredients to oppose venenosity and corroborate the heart. [Nevertheless], many die miserably of it.

And that was the case with poor Thomas.

*Quotations* There will be many occasions when to cite the words of an original source will be more effective than using your own. Quotations can help in several ways. They reinforce the reader's belief in what he is being told, add immediacy to an account or description, convey period atmosphere, and get the historian off the hook of responsibility. For the author too, their use tends to check any tendency to interpret the past too strongly in terms of our present day.

To take an example of reinforcing belief: in the second decade of the eighteenth century, in the London street then known as High Street Cornhill (now just Cornhill), on to which the Royal Exchange then opened, lived Robert Fitzhugh (1682-1754). As a respectable citizen, he was elected to the Cornhill Wardmote. Both his surroundings and his ward activities needed to be described, so I used quotations from the Minute Book of Cornhill's wardmote meetings, which gave a picture both of the discussions in which he took part and of the teeming life of his street. They showed that:

> The hackney coachmen with their coaches do daily pester the High Street of Cornhill. The gentlemen frequenting the Exchange are obstructed in their passage, and stops are often caused in the streets ... Divers hawkers of goods and wares daily frequent the public houses about the Exchange, which is a great detriment to the inhabitants of this Ward ... Numbers of men, women and children do almost daily frequent the end of Castle Alley, adjoining to the Exchange, to hawk and cry newspapers and pamphlets, who are very troublesome to the shopkeepers thereabouts, as [also to] the passengers and gentlemen frequenting the Exchange ... The High Street (as indeed many other parts of the City) are frequently pestered with a loose sort of people who sell fruit and other things in wheelbarrows and permit youth to play with dice for their wares, to the hindrance of the passage through the streets and the corruption of such youth as resort thereto.

Had I described that in my own words, no matter how evocatively, the reader would still have at the back of his mind the reservation: 'Well of course he wasn't actually there.' As it is, the quotation compels belief in the accuracy of the picture.

Description by quotation can create a sense of immediacy by saving the explanations that a reader would expect from an author giving his own account of a situation. In 1756, Thomas Fitzhugh was aboard an East Indiaman when the vessel ran into trouble. Supposing I had the necessary knowledge of sailing a square-rigged ship to be able to describe in my own words the emergency measures taken by the Captain, I should be expected to make them understandable to my landlubber readers. So I let the Captain speak for himself. His logbook of the *Earl of Holderness* reads:

> At half past [ten] we struck upon a sunken rock. We used all the means we could to get her off with our sails, but, that not answering and the tide falling, hove all our guns overboard and everything of weight and started all the water we could come at to lighten the ship; but finding her to lie very uneasy and straining very much obliged us to cut away the mainmast and after it the mizenmast. After which the ship was much easier ... Got all the booms out and made a raft of them. We did not perceive the ship made any water for an hour after she struck, and then she made water very fast [so] that in a little time we had 5 foot water in her hold. Got the chain pumps to work ...

The reader would not expect the Captain to provide him with an explanatory commentary on the urgent measures he was taking.

*Mental atmosphere. The Times* newspaper of 11th March 1815 came out at a time when England was relaxing after what had seemed the victorious conclusion of nearly twenty years of war with France. The tone of the following report must have reflected the frame of mind of the whole nation.

> Early yesterday morning we received by express from Dover the important but lamentable intelligence of a civil war having been again kindled in France by that wretch BUONAPARTE, whose life was so impolitely spared by the Allied Sovereigns. It now appears that the hypocritical villain, who, at the time of his cowardly abdication, affected an aversion to the shedding of blood in a civil warfare, has been employed during the whole time of his residence at Elba in carrying on secret and treasonable intrigues

with the tools of his former crimes in France. At length, when his
plots were ripe, he sailed from Elba . . . and landed near Fréjus in
France on the 3rd instant . . .

Information obtained from newspapers is notoriously suspect. Whenever
possible, check it from another paper and use what they agree upon.
However, it is sometimes a pity to lose a colourful detail supplied by one
reporter merely because another has omitted it; in such a case cover
yourself by quoting the report and attributing it to its source.

The most striking of all quotations is of words spoken, or reported
contemporaneously as being spoken, by an ancestor or someone talking
to him. It cannot fail to convey a strong feeling of intimacy with both the
situation and the person. Imagined dialogues, such as those inserted in
Alex Haley's *Roots* are not history. The most prolific sources of
conversations from long ago are the depositions taken down for use in the
courts of equity and canon law. For examples, see Chapter 11. Sometimes,
for all we can know, the conversations quoted by the witnesses may not be
word-for-word accurately repeated. Indeed, when two deponents quote
the same statement there is often a slight discrepancy, even though their
purport is identical. For instance, in a Chancery case of 1545, two servants
described the arrival at the mistress's house of Thomas Fitzhugh, bringing
the Under Sheriff of Bedfordshire to make an arrest. After some
altercation at the door, the official, according to Katherine Pedder, said:
'Let us do that thing that we came to do', but as quoted by Isabel Wood it
was said as: 'Let us do that thing that we be come for.' When given two
such versions, we have to make a choice. One is sometimes clearer or
more to the point than the other, and therefore the one to use.

To my mind, conversations included in a printed or typed history
should be set out as in a novel, on lines separate from other text. In that
way they will brighten the page and be welcome to those readers who
wonder, like Alice: 'What is the use of a book without pictures or
conversations?'

Pictures we shall come to. First we must deal with some questions that
quotations themselves raise.


*Spelling, capitalisation, punctuation and paragraphing* Until the mid
eighteenth century, spelling was not thought important and was largely
phonetic. Also, in early documents, many written words were started with
a capital letter on no apparent principle. Nouns, especially long or
abstract ones, were often so honoured, and also those of particular interest
to the writer. In logbooks, the word 'ship' was usually given a big S. But the
practice was liable to differ even in the same document. In most old

manuscript records, very little punctuation or paragraphing is to be found, even into the eighteenth century. So for the family historian the decision has to be taken: 'Do I quote exactly as shown in the original, or shall I modernise? And, if the latter, to what extent?'

Many years ago I showed a cousin of mine a transcript I had made of an interesting item of our family history. She, seeing its 'odd' spelling and capital letters, read it aloud with a condescending expression as though it had been written by a small child. That reaction by an ordinarily intelligent 'general reader' made me decide that when I came to write my history all quotations would certainly be modernised in spelling, capitalisation, punctuation and paragraphing. Also, one has only to notice a sign outside Ye Olde Englishe Tea Shoppe to realise that seventeenth-century spelling is regarded as quaint. That again is enough to banish it from my history. Life was never quaint, always real and earnest.

There are, of course, exceptions to every rule. In some documents — probate inventories, for example — an individual type of spelling can indicate a local accent and so perhaps be worth preserving in quotation.

Incidentally, whether you modernise or not, the obsolete letter 'thorn' which was written somewhat like a 'y' (while the real 'y' misleadingly turned its tail the other way) and appears as such on the signs of Ye Olde Englishe Tea Shoppes, should never be represented by a modern 'y' but always by its sound, which was 'th'. Also, the equally obsolete long 's' should never be printed as an 'f'.

Modernising punctuation is not always easy. In long sentences, seventeenth-century writers tended to get their syntax so tangled that modern commas and semi-colons are often powerless to straighten it out. Sometimes the insertion of additional words (always in square brackets, the only way to amend original documents) will do the trick.

Quotations from documents of the late eighteenth century onwards, by which time spelling had become standardised, are, I feel, sometimes exceptions to my above mentioned policy. Unorthodox spelling was by then often evidence of attributes in the writer, such as eccentricity, regional accent or social class, which it might be a pity to iron out by modernisation.

Another modernisation of quotations that I practise is in sums of money. Until the eighteenth century, they were usually expressed in lower case Roman numerals; for example £v. xiijs. iiijd, These look a lot clearer when translated into Arabic numerals as £5.13s.4d.

The limited space available on many old documents did not encourage the luxury of paragraphing; so, in transferring the text to my typed page, I have felt free to be consistent in my modernisation by dividing long quotations into such paragraphs as current usage would require.


*Christian names* In the centuries before ours, people had far fewer Christian names to choose from. Some were, of course, deliberately handed down in a family, but even when a child was christened with a god-parent's name, as was a common practice, the choice was not necessarily widened. The result is that the same names recur generation after generation. In a narrative history this can cause confusion. In one single chapter I have found myself lumbered with three William Fitzhughs, in another with three Marys, and three Roberts. The only way to make clear to whom you are referring is by such devices as 'old William', 'young William', 'William senior', 'William junior', 'William père', 'grandfather William', 'Uncle William' or by mentioning his relationship to the member of the family just spoken of. Americans, taking a leaf out of royalty's book, sometimes use Roman numerals to distinguish themselves from one another, e.g. a distant cousin of mine, Henry Steptoe Fitzhugh II; but that would not do for us — too much like *lèse majesté*. Pet names, all too seldom found in records, can be useful in distinguishing people of the same name. I have been thankful to come across mention of a Tom, son of Thomas, and Bess, servant of Elizabeth.

When this name problem occurs, it is helpful to show a short selective family tree covering the confusing namesakes. Even when there is no identity problem, a brief tree may provide a helpful visual aid. More of that later.


*Money* When sterling currency was decimalised in 1971, there was discussion in historical circles about how to show 'old money'. Some writers recommend the conversion of shillings and old pence into new pence. To me this seemed liable to give the misleading impression that the value too had been updated. Some people would even have liked to do just that, and so convey a meaningful impression of costs. But it would be a very complex and disputatious operation because not all prices have increased in the same degree. Even at the time of writing, house prices in the south of England are rising much faster than in the north and than the price of food. Old money is now usually left in its original form. Occasionally I have thought it needful to add some such comment as: 'That was a lot of money.'

Even though sums of money on the page tend to be meaningless as concerns their value, I believe it is useful for the family historian to mention amounts of wages, salaries or fees paid to or by an ancestor. I once read the biography of an early nineteenth-century English artist, a tradesman's son, who, while still young, untrained and unknown, was described as going off to Italy to study his art, but with no mention of who paid for the journey or how the youth supported himself in Rome. For me, this turned him into an unreal figure gliding effortlessly southward with his feet a few inches above the ground. Such a lack of reality seems to contradict the whole aim of history. Our ancestors' basic requirements, like ours, were food, clothing, shelter and the money to pay for them. So unless you are in a position to say that they were well-off, mentions of their pounds, shillings and pence will help to make them people of bone, flesh and blood. It was reassuring to learn from *Reports on former Monks and Nuns* (PRO.E.101/76/26) that when Thomas Fitzhugh's stepdaughter Alice, a nun, was thrust out into the world at the dissolution of Elstow Abbey in 1538, she received an annual pension from the Crown of £2.13s.4d.

*Dates* Narrative histories usually convert pre-1752 January-March dates into our current Georgian calendar and do it silently. I certainly would never recommend showing a date as '14th February 1696/7'. To readers ignorant of the change in the calendar that would look like uncertainty. I do it, however, for my own reference in my Family Transcripts.

Once, in the 1930s, I took several motorcoach day trips from Penzance to places of historical interest. They were conducted by a retired naval officer who had a cavalier way with dates. For him, and therefore for his listeners, every event in Cornwall between the Old Stone Age and 1914 took place 'in the good old days'. A family historian is more inclined to fall into the opposite error of being over-precise in placing events in time, probably because he is transferring them bodily from his family tree. Dates are, of course, important. Readers like to know where they are on the time scale; so whenever a year changes the new date should be mentioned unobtrusively, but repeating the same year every time an incident occurs sounds pedantic. It is enough to say 'on the 5th May', and once a day and month have already been mentioned, exactness is even less important and the next incident can be timed by some such colloquial phrase as 'a fortnight later'. In my typescript history I have adopted the device of showing the year, or years, at the top of each page, level with the page number (see the sample chapter), so that if ever the reader feels lost it is quicker for him to glance upwards than to hunt backwards through the text.

Being able to identify the day of the week sometimes reveals points not obvious from the dates alone, such as that a parish vestry regularly held their meetings on the first Wednesday of each month. Also it can save repeated mentions of dates by enabling the use of such phrases as 'on the following Saturday', which also conveys a feeling of relaxed intimacy with the situation. In my *Dictionary of Genealogy* I included a Perpetual Calendar, enabling the days of the week to be identified.


*Unity-of-the-Family theme* Although I am writing my history in the role of storyteller and therefore eschewing any view of my ancestors' historical situations wider than I think they would have seen it themselves, there is one type of situation that draws me out of my contemporaneousness — consistency is a minor virtue — and that is the effect that some event long ago continues to have on me and my relatives today. Drawing attention to this acts as a reminder of the unity of the continuing family, and therefore of the history's theme. An example of what I mean is a narrow escape we had in 1599. My ancestor Robert Fitzhugh did not marry his girl friend (and possible betrothed) until a fortnight before the christening of their first child, who was also my ancestor. If Robert had failed to do the gentlemanly thing, our name would not now be FitzHugh but Worsley.

More generally occurring long-term effects are those caused by an ancestor's thrift or improvidence. A marked improvement in the family's fortunes calls for a word of appreciation from an author who is an ultimate beneficiary; and he can be excused for reproaching an ancestor who brought the family to ruin. However, there were some circumstances (land clearance, enclosure, famine) beyond the ability of even the most conscientious breadwinner to cope. When my progress on my history reaches Queen Victoria's reign I shall probably draw attention to how nineteenth-century advances in medical science and sanitary engineering were responsible for endangering the eighteenth-century appreciation in our family fortunes. My grandfather, William Henry FitzHugh, a barrister-civil servant, had a large family of children, and for the first time ever, nine of them flourished to outlive their parents, so that, on his death, his estate was divided into somewhat vulgar fractions.


*Foreign place-names* As the Census Returns and the Canterbury Prerogative Court Will Indexes remind us, many of the people we are researching may have either come into this world or gone out of it in 'foreign parts', and the records of the chartered companies tell us a good deal about their lives. Because of this, we are liable to find ourselves writing about happenings in lands and cities overseas, of which the

English names have since been changed; and what our ancestors called them may be unfamiliar to the young of today, and even more so to those of future generations. In the eighteenth century an ancestor of mine spent his working life in Constantinople, but I am not at all sure that my grandchildren know where that is, or was. Today we call it by the same name as it was known to the Turks even then, Istanbul. In the same way, Ceylon is now Sri Lanka, Persia is Iran, Peking is Beijing. So, which name are we to put in our history, the one our ancestor used or the modern one? My personal decision is to keep true to the spirit of the period by using my ancestor's version, but, on its first mention and then only, to add the present name in brackets.

*Backgrounds to the fore* Our ancestors' careers were not solely the collective outcome of their own activities. As already mentioned, there were impersonal forces that pressed upon them as inhabitants of their locality, members of their trade or profession and subjects of their king. In your record keeping you are likely to have classed these forces as Background Material, and so they are, but some of them can become most interesting foreground stories. During the Civil War the towns of Bristol, Gloucester and Exeter, to name only three, endured sieges. Each was a memorable experience in the lives of all the citizens; so if your family was among them, you should certainly find and give an account of the dangers and privations they experienced. There were also other outside events that struck fear into the hearts of our ancestors, namely the visitations of plague that occurred frequently down to the late seventeenth century, and of cholera, less frequently but equally terrifyingly, in the nineteenth. It is difficult today to imagine the degree of alarm these caused, certainly quite enough to warrant inclusion in your history even though no member of the family died of them. My grandmother, during one cholera visitation, stuck the following cutting from an unidentified late nineteenth-century newspaper into her book of recipes and household hints:

> Cholera is not a very dangerous disease if only the following precautions are taken. Live well; eat no fruit or vegetables of any kind except boiled or baked potatoes. Have no carpets, curtains or waxed floors, and scrub the floors daily with hot — very hot — water, into which has been thrown carbolic acid or some other disinfectant. Throw carbolic acid daily into the drains and dust-bins. Have good disinfectants in every room and renew them daily. Sprinkle the walls with carbolic acid, and if they can be washed with hot water and carbolic acid, all the better. When you go out,

sprinkle your clothes with carbolic acid; avoid cabs, omnibuses and tramways. Drink in moderation water that has been previously boiled, and put into it a tea-spoonful of rum for every glass. When the baker brings the bread, put it into a very hot oven for a few minutes. At the most insignificant indisposition, go to bed if possible and take a cup of hot tea or some other sudorific ...

In this wicked world, divine protection from such visitations could not be altogether relied upon. My great-grandfather, a Sussex clergyman, listened to his Bishop's sermon at Lewes in October 1853. As the *Sussex Advertiser* reported:

The reverend prelate, in delivering his charge to the clergy, churchwardens, etc., spoke of the too great leniency with which society looked upon those sins for which retribution was not provided in our courts of justice ... He alluded to the subject now because of the reappearance of a plague which committed fearful ravages a few years ago ... Though the Almighty in his goodness seemed now for a time to have withdrawn it, they could have no confidence that it would not return with the spring and the recurrence of warm weather.

Epidemics were not the only local disasters that struck at the minds as well as the bodies of whole communities. Riverside parishes were often flooded, and fires would destroy whole areas of half-timbered houses. Descriptions in local newspapers can be quoted with dramatic effect.

Background material may sometimes contain something of interest or even importance which the foreground evidence of an incident has no occasion to mention. In 1590 Robert Fitzhugh was being sued about some land in the Court of Chancery. The plaintiff alleged that he had gained possession of it by forging an endorsement on a deed of conveyance. If Robert lost that case, he would then be liable to indictment on a criminal charge of forgery, so I thought I would have a look to see what penalty would then have hung over him. I found in *Statutes of the Realm* that an Act of 5 Elizabeth, 1562, made forgery of deeds for the possession of land punishable by being 'set upon the pillory in some open market town ... and then to have both his ears cut off and also his nostrils to be slit and cut and seared with an hot iron' as well as forfeiture of the land and imprisonment. For the diligence of my extra research, what could be more rewarding? Fortunately Robert did not lose his case.

## Writing the narrative

*Authentication* of statements about your family is absolutely necessary if your history is to have any critical credibility. The standard method of achieving this is by reference back to the original documents from which the evidence has been derived. There are several methods of doing this. They all start (as mentioned above) by inserting a superior number in the text at the end of each sentence or phrase requiring one, and this refers the reader to the title of the documentary source. Where the methods differ is in the placing of that information. Academic historians particularly interested in the sources like it to be handy in a footnote at the bottom of the same page; but histories written for general readership usually collect such references together in a list either at the end of each chapter or at the end of the book. I place mine at the end of my chapters, but that is only because I am writing and distributing my history as a serial. If ever I get the complete work finished and printed, I may well have all the references at the end of the volume.

To return to the superior numbers in the text: I avoid letting them run into double figures, which could not but be noticeable, by numbering each page's sources separately, and when there is more than one reference to the same source on the same page, I give them the same number, thus shortening the source list by making 'Ibidem' ('the same place') entries unnecessary except when the first source on one page is the same as the last on the page before.

That was my practice until two years ago, but we live now in the twilight of the typewriter. I have gone over to a word processor, and its superior numbers are so small that even double-figures are inconspicuous. Because of this, I now number my references straight through each chapter, eliminating the need for 'Ibids' altogether, and so making the source list even shorter.

I do not supply reference numerals for statements about the historical background culled from published histories. These I cover in the customary way by providing at the end of the book a bibliography of the main historical works upon which I have drawn. I do, however, supply references for background statements drawn from original manuscript sources unlikely to have been used elsewhere.

*Notes* Not all statements can be authenticated satisfactorily by bare references to one or more documentary sources. Some will be the result of deductive processes exercised upon several clues. For the authentication of such statements explanatory Notes are required; but, unless you are writing the 'detective story' type of history, these should not be allowed to clutter up the text. They should be shown in a separate Notes section at the end of the book. My personal practice is to give the usual reference numeral in the text and enter, for example, 'See Note 6', in the references instead of a source title, and in the Notes section explain my deductions as briefly as possible. When I located my ancestor's home in the first house on London Bridge from the Surrey bank and on the upstream side, this was the result of comparing several items of piecemeal evidence; so the explanation (mentioned here in the chapter on The Ancestor as Householder) went into my Notes section.

The interpretation of incomplete evidence is not always easy. Sometimes you will be obliged to say that an incident 'possibly' or 'probably' happened in the way you tell it, and a Note may be required. Occasionally, though the evidence is not cast-iron, the likelihood of an event having happened in any way but one seems so wildly improbable that I state it flatly as having happened that way; but I still supply a Note explaining my reasons.

Though a family history will be written for the eyes of living relatives and their future generations, it will be a poor-spirited family historian who does not aim at a wider than blood readership. To deserve appreciation for its own sake, his history must show a succession of human beings living within and through a series of historical circumstances upon which the family's individual experiences may even cast fresh light. One occasion when my family's predicament gave me a deeper understanding of a historical event came when, nine days before William Fitzhugh was due to pay the annual ground-rent on his building in Philpot Lane, it was destroyed by the Fire of London. His decision to withhold payment, followed by the financial terms he managed to negotiate with the freeholder for re-erection of the building in conformance with the government's new regulations were quite a revelation to me of some of the details of the practical personal consequences of that disaster. One of my family readers too has commented on his fresh realisation, from our ancestor's experiences, of the ordinary Londoner's situation during the Civil War.

*The centre of the town of Frome at the time of William Titford's death in 1801.*

# 15

# A chapter of family history

In 1983 the Institute of Heraldic and Genealogical Studies held a competition for family histories and attracted a large number of entries. The judges awarded the prize to *The Titford Family: Come Wind, Come Weather* by Mr John Titford. This story of a family of west country origins will be published (by Phillimore & Co.) soon after the appearance of this book. In the meantime, Mr Titford has kindly consented to allow a chapter from it to be included here as an example of a thoroughly researched and carefully written work of historiography.

This chapter tells the tale of William Titford as he and his family strove in the eighteenth century to survive against increasingly difficult odds. William's story was not unique to him; it can stand as a typical example of the fate which befell thousands like him as the eighteenth century drew to its close.

## Chapter XII

## "WILLIAM THE CARDMAKER" (c. 1738-1801)

*Frome and Lullington, Somerset*

### COLD CHARITY

*'Am I not Christopher Sly, old Sly's son of Burton*
*Heath; by birth a pedlar, by education a card-maker*
*... by present profession a tinker?'*
(Shakespeare: 'The Taming of the Shrew')

William Titford, born in 1738-9, was a cardmaker, and a literate one, like his father; at his marriage in 1762 to a young lady by the name of Euodias Stark, he signed his name, leaving her to make her little cross. The name 'Euodias' itself was to prove a bit of a challenge even to the literate: an unusual appellation at the best of times — a variation on 'Yved' — it gave constant trouble to the parish clerk in Frome, who seemed to prefer the alternative 'Evadia'; on one occasion he even began writing the name in his register and gave up in despair half-way through.

The occasion of her marriage was not the first time Euodias had been to Frome; nearly twenty years earlier she had tried to put down roots in the town with a signal lack of success. Born in the little village of Lullington, she was baptised there at the exquisite Norman font in the parish church on February 26th, 1737/8, daughter of Benjamin Stark and his wife Mary. The mother died very shortly afterwards, leaving Benjamin with Euodias and her elder sister, Jane, to raise as best he may. In the event, he made two decisions: he would marry again — which he did, to a lady called Elizabeth — and he would leave the picturesque but increasingly decrepit little village nestling against the northern edge of Orchardleigh Park, seeking a better life in nearby Frome.

It was precisely such optimists as poor Benjamin Stark who were hit hardest by the Settlement Act of 1697, still very much in use in the 1740s; the William Titford who had left Frome for Kent in the early years of the eighteenth century had needed settlement certificates in both 1711 and 1745, in order to satisfy the overseers of the poor of Hawkhurst and then Cranbrook that he would be looked after by his original parish of Frome if ever he became destitute.

But a certificate of that sort was precisely what Benjamin Stark did not have; nothing daunted, he crossed the parish boundary into Frome, taking his new wife and two little daughters along with him. Given the way in which the settlement laws of England operated at the period, it would have been less of a problem to cross the Pennines than to travel that short distance into foreign parochial territory as he had just done. Overseers could smell out a potential pauper a few miles away, let alone a family of four, it being their responsibility '... to keep an extraordinary look-out to prevent persons coming to inhabit without certificates, and to fly to the justices to remove them.'[1] They pounced on the Starks with all speed — not because they were yet chargeable to Frome rates as paupers, but because they were 'likely to become chargeable'. Only later — in 1795 — was the law changed to allow intruders to remain wherever they had chosen to live until they actually became a burden on the rates; here, in 1744, anyone without a certificate was subject to the indignity of being escorted, not to say carried bodily, out of the parish by the overworked constable. The Starks had to go.[2]

The bureaucracy was set in motion: Lord Weymouth, who would sign a settlement certificate for William Titford of Kent a year later, was called upon to put his name to an official removal order. The churchwardens and overseers of the poor of the parish of Frome and the churchwardens and overseers of the parish of Lullington were informed that:

> "... Benjamin Stark, Elizabeth his wife, Jane aged about Ten Years and three quarters, Evodiah aged about Six Years his Children by a former Wife ... were in Frome, ... endeavouring there to settle as Inhabitants thereof, contrary to Law, not Having any Way Acquired or Obtained any Legal Settlement therein ..."[3]

The whole family had to be moved and conveyed back whence they had come; how dare they wander around the countryside without permission?

How glad Euodias must have been, then, in 1762, to achieve an official settlement in Frome by marrying a parishioner, William Titford. Now no-one could evict her!

His new wife had brought slightly more to William than abject poverty as a dowry, nevertheless: her grandfather, another Benjamin Stark, had been a clothworker, and we find her, as his administratrix, involved in a transaction of June 24th, 1789, whereby she and her husband William assigned a moiety of the middle part of a messuage called 'Stokes' in Lullington to George French of Frome, clothworker. Grandfather Stark, who died intestate, had himself bought the property in question in 1706 from a certain John Vigor of Hemington, yeoman: it had cost him £18.[4]

So William and Euodias were not penniless, at least up to 1789; poverty would take its time to get them in its clutches. Other problems than financial ones were to beset the newly married couple, however; as the years went by, five of their children — Benjamin, William, Lucy and two others — were to die in infancy. Three had been baptised at St John's (two of them late baptisms), since William, like his brothers Thomas and Charles, was never quite sure how he stood in relation to the Established Church, and seemed not to want to take any chances. One of the infant children they lost died in May of 1771; by all accounts the winter and spring of that year had been brutally cold. On January 16th, Parson James Woodforde, then at the Somerset village of Ansford, wrote in his diary:

"Extreme hard frost with a cutting wind. It was allowed by my Father and Aunt Anne this afternoon that the weather now is as severe as it was in the year 1740 . . ."[5]

Things grew worse rather than better; as late as April 11th Woodforde notes:

"...never such weather known by any person living at present."[6]

The extremes of cold had already carried off Thomas Titford senior on March 15th; William's child was buried at Badcox Lane Baptist Burial Ground on May 14th, and Woodforde's own father, severely affected by the appalling conditions, died just two days later. Brutal times, indeed.

The only other surviving child of William and Euodias was Sarah, baptised in 1763. She had been an eight-month baby herself, and when she married Joseph Starr in May, 1785, it was to be only seven months before their first child, Mary, was baptised at St John's. Others followed, though by the time young George was baptised in 1793, they were at Rook Lane Meeting House. Many worshippers seem to have switched affiliations from chapel to chapel or from church to chapel almost as the whim of the moment took them, just as Joseph and Sarah did here.

Not all the Starrs' children survived, and we read in the Catherine Hill Baptist Burial Register of 'Willm. Titfords 1st and 2d grandc buryd May 6th 1790'. Soon to follow his own children into grave number 80 was Joseph Starr himself; described rather disparagingly as 'Joseph Starr, Titfords son in law' (perhaps William paid for the burial?), he was laid to rest on May 10th, 1796.

The loss of loved ones was to be only one of William's problems: exactly a hundred years after his ancestor, William the Wiredrawer, had improved his fortunes and acquired his eight houses in Fountain Lane, William the Cardmaker found himself on parish relief of 2/- a fortnight, starting on September 27th, 1793. It was a doubtful privilege which he was to enjoy until his death. Wire-drawing had brought the family a degree of wealth in the past, and cardmaking had seemed a safe enough trade in the early and middle years of the eighteenth century. But as that century drew to a close, here was William, soon to be followed into pauperdom by his two cardmaker brothers, on the parish on and off until his weary body gave up the struggle. Only brother Charles, who was a shopkeeper and could raise his prices as his costs rose, managed to avoid the poverty trap —and even then, only just.[7]

There is no shortage of possible explanations as to why William Titford should have ended up in the parochial dole queue in the September of 1793. Harvests had been bad the year before, and 1793 itself was to be a year of international crisis: France declared war on Holland and Britain at the beginning of February, and news from across the channel — that Louis XVI had been guillotined, Marat murdered and the Reign of Terror well underway — must have sent a frisson of horror down many an English spine.

At home, the closing decades of the century were cruel ones for all wage-dependent people as a '... vast flood of pauperism was beginning to engulf almost the whole of the labouring classes'.[8] Some artisans could just keep their heads above water, possibly by resorting to the dual occupations so much favoured by many of their sixteenth- and seventeenth-century forebears; Frome's James Trotman, for example, a cardmaker like William Titford, spread his risks by taking up a little side-line as a dealer in earthenware. For those not so enterprising or so lucky, accepting the parish dole was frequently the only alternative.

By 1781-2 and the passing of Gilbert's Act, it was becoming increasingly clear that the workhouses could never accommodate the sheer numbers of new paupers being created day-by-day; the new act entitled able-bodied men to parish relief for the first time — if only in augmentation of existing bread-line wages. The cash pension was thereafter to become the universal remedy to combat widespread poverty, as a statute of 1796 widened the scope of the Gilbert provision and overseers were allowed to order outdoor relief without applying the workhouse test. Not only that but, mercifully, paupers' badges need no longer be worn publicly, '... upon proof of very decent and orderly behaviour'.[9]

By the time Sir Frederick Norton Eden visited Frome in the middle 1790s, he noted that the new legislation was being complied with:

"The poor are chiefly maintained at home, where it is thought they can be relieved at less expense to the parish than if they were sent to the workhouse."[10]

If Eden is right here, it does give an interesting slant to the problem, of course; in his view outdoor relief had replaced admission to the workhouse from motives of parish parsimony, not humanity ....

So William Titford's situation as a parish-subsidised pauper must be seen against a fairly desperate local and national back-drop. Other personal factors may also have come into play: he may have been sick or injured — though the overseers would probably have noted the fact in their accounts; he may have been ready for what we should today think of as an old-age pension — it was nothing unusual for a man to 'retire' when he reached fifty, prematurely aged by a strenuous life, a limited diet and poor medical care. William, in the event, was aged fifty-four, certainly approaching the end of his active life. Yet if we look closely enough, we can find what may prove to be the most likely explanation for his enforced redundancy. In 1794 an ominous advertisement appeared in the *Salisbury Journal*: Rawlings, the firm of Frome card-makers, were pleased to announce that they had now installed a card-making machine. There was still a host of cardmakers in the town at the end of the century, but very many fewer than there had been in the good old days of the early 1700s. At a time of slow but steady decline in the industry, and just as machines were being brought in to do the job, William may well have found, in his middle fifties, that his services were no longer required. All of that makes him, if true, an early victim of the march of technology which would eventually spell the final demise of cloth-making in the town during the next century, as Yorkshire with its modern methods cornered the market

How William survived on a mere pittance of 2/- per fortnight we can only guess at: did he receive any further payment in kind, was there access to subsidised food, could his family and friends help out in any way?[11]

Five years later, in the May of 1798, William's wife

Euodias joined her husband on the list of paupers; she was not to be there long. Her 1/- per fortnight benefit, a supplement to the 3/- he was by then receiving, stops abruptly in mid-summer; the Catherine Hill sexton had another job to perform —'Willm Titfords wife' was buried on August 16th, no longer a burden on the ratepayers. The overseers promptly reduced William's fortnightly benefit to 2/6d on August 21st — no point in paying a man for a dependant he no longer had . . ..

We might spare a thought for William Titford here in the summer of 1798; his plight was obviously not untypical, but hard enough for all that. Aged sixty, a widower; five children dead in infancy, one daughter widowed; he himself trying to keep body and soul together on a mere half-a-crown a fortnight, his brothers nearly as poor as he, and prices rising month by month. His own end — mercifully, we may say —was not to be long delayed. By 1800 he was living in a house on the west side of High Street, owned by John Imber, a woolstapler — very probably the same house that Thomas his father had built the year before William was born. Quite a short street, then as now, it consisted mainly of houses or houses and gardens, except for Thomas Imber's workshops on the same side as William.

Here William continued to receive poor relief; various amounts of 1/3d, 2/- and even 4/- were paid, according to need or the overseers' moods. By 1800 the end was already near, as payments became stablished at 2/- per week until October 27th, 1801. Then, perfunctorily: 'Dead'.

It cost the parish 11/6d to bury poor William; he was the first of the four brothers to go, and no doubt they mourned him, though Charles, at least, was already ill and very near his own death at the time, and Thomas was to live only two years longer.

Perhaps the greatest indignity for William was that even in the grave there was no rest; nearly six years later, in the July of 1807, he and one other body were dug up to make room for a younger twenty-two year old corpse, that of William's grand-daughter, Mary Starr. What price the Age of Enlightenment?

# References

[1] Burn, *History of the Poor Law*, p.121. Quoted in Tate, *The parish chest*, p.197.

[2] 1744 was a bad year generally for those who fancied a change of scenery and a fresh parish of residence; it saw the passing of an act (17 Geo III c.5) whereby a justice was empowered to have vagrants conveyed, after interrogation, to the place of their last legal settlement.

[3] Details from the original Removal Order, Longleat House archives, Box 31.

[4] Details from Orchardleigh Muniments SRO. Ref. DD/DU 14.

[5] James Woodforde, *The diary of a country parson*, Ed. John Beresford. Oxford University Press paperback, 1978, p.70.

[6] *Ibid*, p.73. Another excellent source for the extremes of late eighteenth-century weather is Gilbert White, *The natural history of Selborne*, available in many editions including that edited by Richard Mabey for Penguin Books, 1977. White talks of the frost in January, 1768, as being 'the most severe that we had then known for many years . . . the Thames was at once so frozen over both above and below bridge that crowds ran about on the ice' (op.cit., pp.253, 259). Predictably, two Titford deaths followed almost immediately: William lost a child who was buried on February 9th, and Thomas Titford's second child was buried on February 24th.

[7] *A pyramid of society in the United Kingdom* by Patrick Colquhoun, reflecting social classes at the end of the Napoleonic Wars, places 'Shopkeepers and Hawkers' surprisingly high in the structure, above Master Craftsmen and Manufacturers, Lesser Freeholders, Farmers and Teachers, Actors, Clerks and Shopmen. Only then do we come across the category which would include cardmakers: 'Artisans and other skilled workers'. He calculates that shopkeepers and their dependents numbered 600,000, with artisans at 4,500,000. Perhaps he is thinking here of more grand shopkeepers than a humble butcher and cheesemonger like Charles Titford? For details, see G.D.H. Cole and Raymond Postgate, *The common people, 1746-1946*, Methuen, 1976.

[8] W.E. Tate, *The parish chest*, p.80.

[9] *Ibid*, p.194.

[10] Sir Frederick Norton Eden, *The state of the poor*, 1797. Quoted in Michael McGarvie, *Frome through the ages*, Frome Society for Local Study, 1982, p.106.

[11] As an indicator of just how little 2/6d. per fortnight might have been in real terms in the late eighteenth century, we might look at a table of wages for the period which appears in Cole and Postgate's *The common people*, p.76. It gives the daily wage of a craftsman ('chiefly skilled building operatives') in the west of England in 1790 as 2/4d. In other words, William Titford was trying to survive on almost the same sum per *fortnight* as other craftsmen were earning *per day*.

# 16

# Illustrations

Illustrations are more than mere embellishments to a family history. No words can describe a Victorian grandfather's appearance as correctly or vividly as a photograph; still less can they convey any impression of Grandmama in her 'leg-of-mutton' sleeves and 'teapot handle' coiffure. (Younger readers, read Great-Grandpa and Great-Grandma; your grandparents are likely to be still around, and in jeans.)

## Portraits of the family

Studio portrait photographs date from 1841. Photographs taken at customers' own homes soon followed. I have some family groups from the early 1850s taken outdoors with a sheet rigged up to make a plain background, but with its edges just showing. It includes my great-great-grandmother, born in 1767, her granddaughter, who died in 1933, and the generation between them. From that time on, in many families, *carte de visite* studio portraits become more and more numerous. Too often they have no sitter's name on the back, though some have passed down the family with oral identification. All oral tradition, however, needs to be treated with caution. *Family Tree Magazine* carried an amusing story of a three-quarter length photograph of Queen Alexandra *en grande tenue*, once on popular sale, but which had been passed down to its present owner as 'Aunt Ann, who was jilted and went a bit funny'. How much more likely it is for one real member of the family to be mistaken for another.

Many of these portrait photographs survive in old albums. For family history purposes each should be rephotographed, the copy mounted on a sheet of your Family Transcript paper and inserted in the binder in its chronological order. There it ceases to be a Portrait of a Dead Relative and becomes an illustration to his or her life, and in due course will give your history all the more impact.

Dating an old portrait photograph is not always easy, even if the sitter is known. If the name and address of the photographer is shown, it is possible to discover the dates between which he was in business at that

*A rare photograph of a man — a centenarian — born in the reign of George II.*

178

place from local directories or from the Royal Photographic Society's published series of directories of photographers. Where no photographer's name is indicated, an approximate date can be estimated from the sitter's dress style (male or female) with the assistance of C.W. & P. Cunnington's lavishly illustrated *Handbook of English Costume in the Nineteenth Century*. Even when the photographer's dates are known, costume style can help to place the portrait nearer to the precise year. Fashions however can only be relied on for an earliest date. Family groups can often be dated by estimating the apparent approximate age of each member of the group, and working out a date compatible with them all and with any known facts that are relevant.

If the date of any photograph, or indeed of any illustration whatever, is known, it should always be indicated. This is, of course, particularly important when they have been taken by someone at a considerable remove from the period they illustrate, such as by yourself.

*A carte de visite photograph, the most popular form of Victorian studio portraiture. The name and address of the photographer on the back, taken with the dress and hairstyle of the sitter and family data, would enable this picture to be fairly closely dated.*

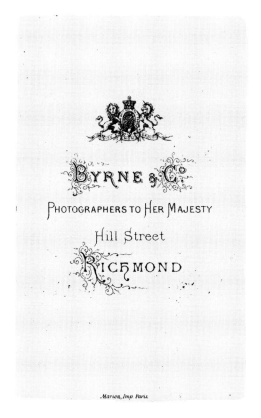

179

*Picture postcards pasted into family albums may be there because they show the family home. This picture is of Wigton, Cumbria, about 1900.*

Faded photographs, when rephotographed and printed on high-contrast paper can reproduce the sharpness of the original, often to an astonishing degree. Several photographers now advertise this service in genealogical journals.

Any painted portraits or miniatures of members of the family should of course be photographed in colour, and the prints inserted in the Family Transcript binder in their appropriate place.

## *Family environment*

Many libraries and record offices have collections of photographs and picture postcards of localities dating back to Victorian times. With luck it may even be possible to find one that includes an ancestral home. In any case, the family's surroundings will be of interest. Copies of these can usually be purchased. The same repositories are likely to have local topographical pictures from before the photographic era. I have a copy of Hollar's drawing of Old London Bridge. All it shows of my ancestor's home is the roof, but the Bear Inn next door and the bridge itself with its gatehouse, are shown as seen from a non-existent hilltop just to the south.

An imaginary high view-point was popular with topographical artists and mapmakers until well into the eighteenth century.

## Events

Over the last hundred and thirty-odd years certain historical events involving numbers of our ancestors, especially wars, have been given considerable pictorial coverage. I have copies of photographs relevant to my family dating from the Crimean War of 1854-6, through the Second Afghan and Indian Frontier wars, to World Wars I and II. The early ones tend to look static because of the photographic exposure time required at that period, but journals such as the *Illustrated London News* carried artists' impressions of battles and other events which are full of action, though of course a good deal less reliable.

Satirical cartoons or serious drawings of situations in which my ancestors were involved have also not been difficult to find: the 'virtues' of Puritanism contrasted with the 'vices' of Anglicanism, the Plague and Fire of London, the Thames docks, East Indiamen lying off foreign ports,

*A family album picture showing King Edward VI in a horse-drawn coach may be there because the event took place in the ancestor's town — local newspapers can help here —or because the ancestor or his house is shown in the picture.*

181

*George Cruikshank caricatures the difficulties experienced by census enumerators in an age when households of extended families and numerous servants were common.*

English traders in the Levant, the native Caribs of St Vincent, and several political caricatures by Gilray and Cruikshank of controversies during one ancestor's period as a Member of Parliament.

Most of these illustrations I have found without looking for them. For years I have subscribed to *History Today*, where I have come across the bulk of them. I cut them out and insert them in their appropriate places in my Family Transcript volumes. The provenance by-line of each is noted so that I know where to apply — and whom to pay — for any originals that I select for reproduction in my final printed history. I should like to include them all, but I have far too many, even for a coffee-table book.

## *Maps*

When I was a boy, my aunts asked me what kind of book I liked best, and I said: 'Ones with a map', which resulted in my getting two copies of *Treasure Island* that Christmas. I still feel a strong attraction to maps as a vivid and effective visual aid in a family history, but they must be as nearly as possible contemporary with the generation for which they are being used. Copies can be obtained from print libraries or ordinary libraries, or county or borough record offices. I have collected a number of

*Beware of making assumptions from photographic evidence. The child* TOP LEFT *is a boy, not a girl. The 'cyclists' were photographed against a painted backdrop in a studio for an advertisement. However, no lady of the Victorian period would have been photographed showing so much leg as does Mary Ann Pansa* RIGHT *unless she genuinely was on the stage.*

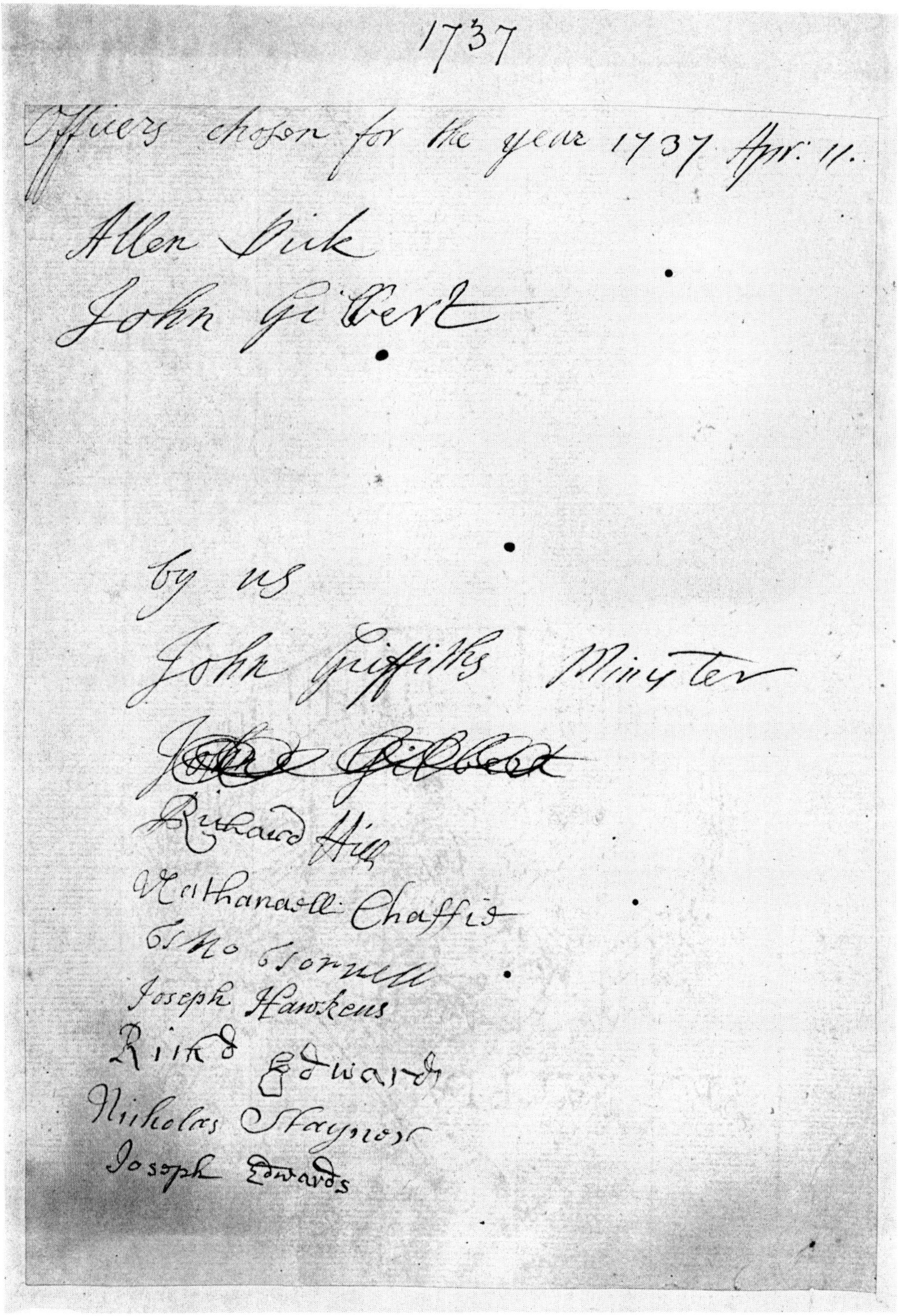

1737

Officers chosen for the year 1737 Apr. 11.

Allen Dick
John Gilbert

by us

John Griffiths Minister

~~John Gilbert~~

Richard Hill

Nathanaell Chaffie

Tho Cornell

Joseph Hawkens

Rich'd Edward

Nicholas Naynor

Joseph Edwards

relevant ones dating from Speed's work of 1610 onwards. The availability of reprints of early nineteenth-century Ordnance Survey maps from Messrs David & Charles is a great help.

With my family involvement in early eighteenth-century voyages, my searches for relevant maps have extended to old maritime charts of coastal areas. These were often decorated with sketches of ships and relevant port towns. My sea-captain ancestor frequently had difficulty when navigating the approach to the Hooghly River in India, with its submerged and shifting sandbanks, so I have a photographic copy of just such a chart as he himself must have used. This and others I obtained from the National Maritime Museum, Greenwich.

## Ancestral autographs

I have made an illustration from some of these by cutting the signatures out of photocopies of signed documents, mounting several of them on one sheet of paper and typing in the identity of the persons concerned, with their birth and death years and the date of each signature. I have also added a note to explain that two of them were in Secretary Hand. Any dirt or age marks from the original document that have been reproduced in the photocopy I have removed with a typists' correction fluid. I have then had the finished sheet bearing the autographs and their captions rephotocopied.

## Family trees

Obviously the family that is the subject of the history must have its tree shown, and the author may like to add trees of any collateral branches. These, however, will usually be included as appendices rather than as illustrations in the text. However, readers cannot be expected to keep all the members of the family in their memory, so occasionally visual aids are needed in the shape of short selective trees showing just those members whose positions are currently needing clarification. Such a tree is quite likely to include the issue of two or more siblings, which can make a very large number of people to find horizontal room for on the page. The following is an example of a selective tree showing one way of dealing with this layout problem:

*Examples of an ancestor's handwriting, and particularly of his signature, are intimate items of evidence. Among these appointees of churchwardens in 1737, Richard Edwards was evidently one of the eldest, since he wrote in the by then outmoded Secretary Hand.*

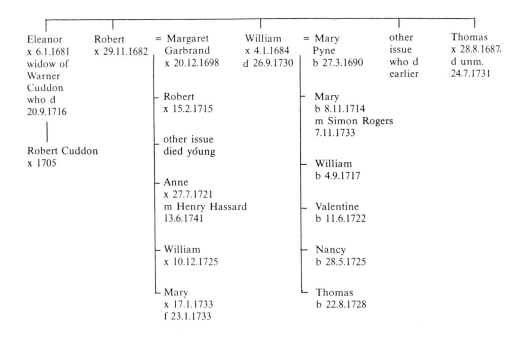

When laying out a family tree in typescript it is particularly helpful to be able to use only single-letter abbreviations for all the 'vital' events. My answer to this problem is contained in the following table:

| | | | | | | | | |
|---|---|---|---|---|---|---|---|---|
| b | = | born | p | = | probate | f | = | funeral |
| d | = | died | x | = | christened (baptised) | m | = | married |
| k | = | killed | c | = | circa | w | = | will made |

There is nothing arbitrary about my two innovations, *f* and *x*, which do away with the difficulty caused by *b* standing for *born* and therefore causing longer abbreviations for *baptism* and *burial*. Burial is already almost entirely a thing of the past, having given way to cremation; so *bur* will cease to be appropriate as from this present generation. The initial *f* for *funeral* conveniently covers both kinds of disposal of the body, and funeral is anyway the term always actually used. *X* (which is not really the English letter between *w* and *y*, but the Greek letter *Chi*) has for centuries been the traditional abbreviation for Christ, e.g. in Xmas and Xopher; so it is the natural one-letter abbreviation for *christened*. Showing the dates of will-making and probate, unless of course the deceased was intestate, is already the customary usage for indicating an approximate date of death when actual dates of neither death nor burial are known.

186

# 17

# Titles and other subjects

## *Titles*

Choosing a title for a family history requires careful thought and consideration for others. Most people want the name of their family to appear on the title page, but for many that is not enough; their history has a theme that gives it more than mere family interest, and they wish to announce it on the dust jacket. Continuing in the principle to which this book is committed, of providing actual examples, I have picked for this purpose a number of family history titles from recent Accessions lists in the *Genealogists' Magazine*. I have read none of the histories themselves, and am discussing solely their titles as indications of their contents. They fall into four separate categories and within each category subtle differences distinguish them.

Those in the simplest group differ in wording, but all contain the family name either in the singular or plural; seven add just the word *family*, of which two acknowledge that there are other families of the same name; five explain that the contents are a *history*, with the remaining three preferring *story, book* and *papers* respectively. *Papers* carries a nice suggestion of a family muniment chest. As an exercise, you might try substituting your name in each of these title styles:

### The Plain

| | |
|---|---|
| *The Chamberlains* | D.H. Elletson |
| *The Tatler family* | C.R. & A. Tatler |
| *The family Courtier* | D.B. Courtier |
| *The Puttenham/Puttnam/Putnam family* | Norman Graham |
| *The Askew Family to 1868* | Jack Bloomfield |
| *Bradshaw and related families* | Evelyn M Wright |
| *A Swan family* | William Swan |
| *A branch of the Gompertz family* | R.M. Gompertz |
| *A history of the Cadbury family* | J.F. Crosfield |
| *The history of the Amsden family* | Peter C. Amsden |
| *Flood family history from St Catherine's House* | J. Flood |

## Titles and other subjects

| | |
|---|---|
| *Hilliard family history* | E.H. Hilliard |
| *The Batemans — a family history* | Roger Bateman |
| *The Westbrook story* | Gwen Morgan |
| *The Bater Book and Allied families* | A.L. Bowerman |
| *The Rolfe Papers* | V.P. Brentwood |

All except the Swans and Gompertzes might, by other families of the same name (supposing there are any), be considered somewhat arrogant. Even those two do not make clear which Swans and Gompertzes they are, an omission that the histories in the next list take some pains to avoid.

### The Specific

| | |
|---|---|
| *The Brownes of London* | R. Brown |
| *Waterworth: the story of a Lancashire family* | A.F. Waterworth |
| *The Martin family of Stithians in Cornwall* | E.A. Martin |
| *Argent of Bethnal Green and Hampstead* | J. & R. Newland |
| *The family of Pinches, the medallists* | J.H. Pinches |
| *The Goggs family: Norfolk farmers* | J.F. Fone |
| *A Huguenot family Le Blond* | Marie Bennett |

Identifying a family by locality seems the most popular method, but for families who moved house from one generation to another that may not be possible. Occupation comes next, but how many families are lucky enough to have a continuously inherited skill or commercial business? The Goggses use both methods of identification. Huguenots of a given surname may well know they all descend from one immigrant ancestor.

### The Romantic

| | |
|---|---|
| *The Fighting Forsters* | Joe Forster |
| *The Shervingtons: soldiers of fortune* | K. Shervington |

Presumably these titles do distinguish the families from others by their personal characteristics. 'Oh good afternoon, Mr Forster. How interesting to meet you. One of the fighting family, I presume.' 'Well, er, no, I'm afraid I'm one of the peaceable lot.' 'Nothing to be ashamed of, Mr Forster; nothing at all. Oh, hello, George!' The author was wise not to localise the family. *The Fighting Forsters of Fittleworth* would have sounded like public-house brawlers.

### The Imaginative

| | |
|---|---|
| *A Goodly Heritage* [Baines] | Leslie Baines |
| *A North Devon family* [Dark] | Arthur Dark |
| *Genesis and Exodus* [Benson] | David Williams |
| *Kapana: A Place on the River* [Barraclough] | L. Barraclough & J. Smith |
| *Across the Years* [Gilberd] | E.B. Gilberd |

Titles like these, in which no family name is mentioned, are presumably considered by their authors to have some other strong claim to interest, but do their titles convey this to potential readers? *A Goodly Heritage* sounds a comfortable read. *A North Devon Family* has pleasant local connotations. *Across the Years* conveys the impression of a history, but not much more. *Genesis and Exodus* is puzzling, and *Kapana*, the place on the unnamed river, seems deliberately mysterious.

Not one of the ideas inherent in any of the above titles helps me with my own difficulty. I want a title to express so many different aspects of my history that there is little hope of cramming them all onto one book spine. At night I suddenly think of just the right thing, and drop off to sleep with the whole problem solved; but in the morning I wonder what ever I saw in it. The one I like best is the one I thought of first, but my relations all say: 'Oh no, not that!' Still, I am not mentioning it here in case one of you takes it and I shall be left with nothing. Anyway, publishers have their own ideas about titles, because a good name can sell a book —names like:

> *We Came with the Conqueror*
> *From Ploughboys to Plutocrats*
> *My Claim to the Throne*

Seriously, though, those words on the cover are not to be chosen lightly.

## Collateral branches

In the course of genealogical research into your own branch of the family, you will almost certainly have discovered one or more collateral branches descending from your ancestors' brothers. Life is not long enough for researching the family history of all those branches in addition to your own, but you may well like to show the genealogy of the whole extended family in one or more family trees; and your distant cousins will almost certainly be glad to see themselves mentioned and be motivated to buy a copy. Some may even be stimulated by your achievement to research the lives of their own lines.

The inclusion of trees of all known collateral branches makes clear the known limits of your extended family, and that will help genealogists of the same surname but different origins to narrow their field of research. It may also have the opposite effect of enabling a reader to prove membership of a surviving collateral branch of your family hitherto unknown to you.

When I complete my history, I shall certainly add an Appendix showing an extended tree of all the FitzHughs in Great Britain. I should very much like to include all the branches abroad but that would mean creating a second volume. My ancestor's cousin who emigrated to Virginia in 1674 had twelve children; his sons followed with equally numerous issue, and the fertility of the American stock continued down the generations, so that today my living Fitzhugh cousins in the USA (spelling themselves with a small 'h') number many hundreds, perhaps even thousands.

When planning an Appendix of collateral family trees, there are three different kinds to consider: (1) those lines still surviving; (2) those that you know for certain have died out; (3) those you have lost track of, which may or may not have representatives living today. Will you have room to include all three types? If not, presumably those in category one will be those with the greatest right to be included, and those in two the first to be sacrificed.

## Other families of the same name

Members of other families of the same surname, when they learn of your successful researches, are certain to write to you, hoping that you can assist them with their enquiries. Inevitably in your genealogical researches, you will have come across strangers of your name and made notes of them all until you could be quite sure that they were people of a different stock. You may even have joined a One-Name Society and exerted yourself to collect all documentary mentions of the same surname. So it will save trouble, for enquirers and yourself, if your Appendix includes a brief mention of other families of your name, together with their early habitats and your reasons for disclaiming any connection with them.

# 18

# Reaching readers

When the final chapter of the family history and all the appendices have at last been written, the historian faces a completely new set of problems: how to make copies for all the people who he hopes will want to read it; how to do it at a price they are likely to be prepared to pay; and how to do it in a format that will endure the wear and tear of an unpredictable succession of future generations of the family.

Most historians will expect a sale to at least every present adult member of his extended family, plus a presentation copy to the Society of Genealogists and the statutory copies for the copyright libraries. In my experience some relatives with several children and an eye to the needs of eventual collateral descendants will want a copy for each of their offspring. A readership of no more than this extent, perhaps fifty copies, will call for a certain set of methods for supplying the demand, while an edition running into thousands will have to be handled altogether differently. First, we will consider the more modest ambition.

*Subscription list* Before you launch into production it is best to find out from members of your family how many copies they will want to buy. They will expect you to let them know the price, so you will first have to consider the expense of the required production stages. Costing them will be a chicken-and-egg problem, because some of the charge will vary according to the number of copies involved. The best you may be able to do is to quote your prospective customers a price range, plus postage and packing. This will result in a subscription list that will give you something on which to base your plans.

*Printing* Modern typewriters and word processors, capable of using several types of lettering and of 'justifying' lines so that they do not leave a ragged right-hand margin, can now produce a very professional-looking text; and Letraset, or similar proprietary adhesive lettering systems, make possible the production of attractive title pages and chapter headings.

*Size of page* For a hardback volume, A4 page size is unwieldy to handle and too large to fit into many bookcases. A5, half the size of A4, has about the same dimensions as most books, but if the text on it has been reduced in size by photocopying, the lettering is too small for comfortable reading. A good compromise is to have two pages of text copied side by side, with slight reduction, onto B4 paper. The resulting page size is 10 x 8 inches (the old quarto size), still somewhat larger than most books, but perhaps appropriately so for a volume of such special personal interest.

*Copies* For convenience with quality, modern sophisticated photocopiers with their capability to enlarge and reduce, and to reproduce colour and photographs on ordinary paper, offer the most economical method of reproducing illustrated texts in limited quantity. Even so, many family historians or their relations will be working for firms that have photocopiers of their own; so they may be able to arrange to use them for their history at cost price or a special reduced rate. After all, the shop charge for photocopying is about ten times the actual cost.

*Bookbinding* Any arrangement for typing several medium-sized pages onto large sheets of paper involves taking into consideration in advance the method of book-binding to be used. Needless to say, looseleaf ring-binders are not to be thought of; and nor is the so-called 'perfect binding', which applies adhesive to the inner edges of assembled separate sheets. This is insufficiently durable for a book intended to pass intact down to future generations. For lasting strength, the pages need to be thread-sewn together in batches of sixteen (four folded B4 sheets). This means that they must be typed (or stuck) onto the sheets in a special order. In the folded batch, the outside B4 sheet must bear pages 1 and 16 on its outer sides, and 2 and 15 on the inner. The next sheet will have pages 3 and 14 on its outside, and 4 and 13 inside; and so on, until pages 8 and 9 meet in the middle of the batch.

Bookbinding is a skill that one can learn at evening classes, but applying it to up to fifty volumes is not a project many people would cheerfully face. It is better to search telephone directory 'Yellow Pages' for a professional bookbinder, and pay for it to be expertly done. Leather may appeal as the material of the most suitable dignity for a family history, but it is both expensive and unsuitable. Without the regular application of lanolin preparations, a leather binding will in time (a century or so) crack where the front cover joins the spine; so a cloth binding on boards is in every way the better choice.

*Illustrations* Family trees, maps and many pictures can be reproduced excellently by photocopiers. These should be placed on your B4 sheets of typescript as described above, so that after folding they will appear close to the subject they illustrate. Any photographs or paintings that are beyond photocopying capability will have to be rephotographed, and the prints stuck onto pages left blank for that purpose except for the appropriate caption. Any illustration obtained from an outside source may be copyright, so that, in addition to the charge made for making you a copy, a reproduction fee will be due if it is used in a publication of any kind. The fact that the original picture may be in, or have come from, a printed book that has long been in the public domain does not necessarily exempt its use from this fee. Maps, too, are subject to reproduction fees. All published modern maps, from whatever publisher, are based on originals by the Ordnance Survey, to whom negotiable reproduction fees are payable if copies of your family history are to be circulated.

*Titling* The professional who binds the book will also apply the title to its spine. In order to prevent this process from becoming an expensive item, it is best to order a zinc die, in a chosen type of lettering, from a die stamper (Yellow Pages again), and supply it to the binder for his use.

*Cost* The cost to the family historian of producing enough copies to supply his family may amount to as much as £500, a little more than a video recorder or somewhat less than a holiday for two; and he can expect to recover some or all of it from members of his family at a cost to each of them of a restaurant meal for a couple. If, however, the historian wishes his work to be in conventional print and issued to the public at large, he will have to approach a publisher and be prepared for an outlay of several thousand pounds.

The history of an 'ordinary' family is unlikely to hold out hopes of anything like enough sales to interest an 'ordinary' commercial publisher. There are, however, certain specialist publishers who offer services to family historians intent on getting the result of their labours before the public. These start with the preparation of a pre-publication prospectus leaflet for circulation to potential purchasers, offering the volume at a discount price in return for advance commitment to buy. This aims at producing the subscription list, and perhaps some sponsorship from a well-heeled member of the family. The response will reveal how great a deficit the author will have to make good from his own pocket if the project is to go ahead. A really business-like family historian would, I suppose, open a unit trust publication fund at the very commencement of his or her researches, but how many of us prowlers in record repositories run our ancestral obsession on business-like principles?

Once assured of the cost of production, the publisher will enter into a contract with the author to endeavour to sell the unsubscribed copies through relevant retail outlets and his catalogue mailing list. Should sales exceed everybody's hopes, the author may even obtain some partial return of his original deposit, though it would be unwise of me to recommend this system of circulation.

I have mentioned a procedure that I adopted of writing and distributing my family history simultaneously, and this may interest any other family historians who, like me, started on their written opus late enough in life to make it a question, since conscientious progress is so slow, as to whether or not it would ever be completed. I decided to write my family history as a serial and distribute it to the family episode by episode. This affords me a recurring sense of gratification as each successive chapter reaches its public. My instalments have now been maintaining readers' interest in our history for several years, a widening of awareness that itself has given rise to several fresh discoveries.

As each chapter of my history is completed, at about four-monthly intervals, I make two photocopies and post one to a member of the family in England, enclosing a strip of adhesive labels addressed to the other relations on my readership list. This first recipient makes her own photocopy and sends the first copy on to the reader at the top of the address strip. The second recipient does the same, and so on. Many of the addressees take off several copies for their family. The last on the list lets me know that the round has been completed. My second photocopy I send to a distant cousin in America, who has a photocopier of his own and issues the chapters at cost price to others over there.

While this method of continuously alternating attainment and renewal is wonderful for maintaining high morale on the long trek, it does not of course exempt me from the eventual need to make available an enduring hardback edition. My descriptions here of how to go about that final procedure are based not on personal experience, but on information from those in a position to know. However, a glance along the shelves of the Family History section of the Society of Genealogists' library will show how many different results can be achieved by alternative methods. Thanks to modern copying technology, the cost of producing handsome family history volumes for all the family has brought the crowning achievement of a lifetime hobby within the means of most enthusiasts.

# Appendix

## Sources and records mentioned in this book, and some of the places where they may be found.

### Addresses

Borthwick Institute of Historical Research, St Anthony's Hall, University of York, York
British Library, British Museum, Great Russell Street, London WC1
British Library Newspaper Library, Colindale Avenue, London NW9
Corporation of London Record Office, Guildhall, Gresham Street, London EC2
Federation of Family History Societies, 31 Seven Star Road, Solihull, West Midlands B91 2BZ
General Register Office, St Catherine's House, 10 Kingsway, London WC2
Greater London Record Office, 40 Northampton Road, London EC1
Guildhall Library, Aldermanbury, London EC2
House of Lords Record Office, Houses of Parliament, London SW1
India Office Library & Records, Orbit House, Blackfriars Road, London SE1
National Army Museum, Royal Hospital Road, Chelsea, London SW3
Public Record Office, Chancery Lane, London WC2
Public Record Office, Portugal Street, London WC2
Public Record Office, Ruskin Avenue, Kew, Surrey
Society of Genealogists, 14 Charterhouse Buildings, London EC1M 7BA

### Sources and their locations

*Acts & Ordinances of the Interregnum* major reference libraries
*Additional Manuscripts* British Library MSS Department
*Annual Register* Public Record Office, Kew; major reference libraries
*armed services records* Public Record Office, Kew
*army officers' records* Public Record Office, Kew
*army war diaries* Public Record Office, Kew
*assizes records* Public Record Office, Chancery Lane
*Baptist archives* Public Record Office, Chancery Lane; Baptist Union Library, The Angus Library, Regents Park College, Oxford
*bishops' transcripts* county record offices
*borough ward records* borough, city and county record offices
*Bridge House Committee, Journal of* Corporation of London Record Office
*-- Rental Books of* Corporation of London Record Office
*Burney Collection of Newspapers* British Library
*Calendar of Patent Rolls* Public Record Office, Chancery Lane
*census returns* Public Record Office, Portugal Street and Chancery Lane
*certificates of birth/death/marriage* General Register Office
*certificates of residence* Public Record Office, Chancery Lane
*church terriers* county record offices
*churchwardens' accounts* county record offices
*City Freemen records* Clerk of the Chamberlain's Court, Guildhall, London EC2
*City Poor Rate Assessments* Guildhall Library MSS Department
*close and patent rolls* Public Record Office, Chancery Lane
*Congregationalist archives* Public Record Office, Chancery Lane; county record offices; Congregational Library, Memorial Hall, Farringdon Street, London EC4; New College Library, Hampstead, London NW1
*constables and surveyors of highways accounts* county record offices
*conveyance deeds deposited* county record offices

*coroners' inquest records* county record offices
*Court of Assistants, minute books* Guildhall Library MSS Department
*directories, eighteenth-century* Guildhall Library; Victoria & Albert Museum, Cromwell Road, London SW7; Society of Genealogists; county libraries
*-- local* Guildhall Library; Victoria & Albert Museum, Cromwell Road, London SW7; Society of Genealogists
*Drapers Company records* Guildhall Library MSS Department
*East India Company records* India Office Library & Records
*East India House correspondence* India Office Library & Records
*East India ship's logbook and journal* India Office Library & Records
*ecclesiastical court records* county record offices
*equity court records* Public Record Office, Chancery Lane
*estate accounts* county record offices
*Estate Duty records* Public Record Office, Chancery Lane
*family history journals* Society of Genealogists; county family history societies
*Fishmongers Company Freemens List* Guildhall Library
*freeholders' lists* county record offices
*Gentleman's Magazine, The* British Library; Society of Genealogists
*grants of arms* College of Arms, Queen Victoria Street, London EC4V 4BT
*guide books, nineteenth-century* county record offices
*hearth tax lists* Public Record Office, Chancery Lane
*Heralds Visitations* College of Arms, Queen Victoria Street, London EC4V 4BT
*-- Harleian Society editions* major reference libraries
*History of Parliament* major reference libraries
*Hudsons Bay Company records* Public Record Office, Kew
*inheritance taxes* Public Record Office, Chancery Lane
*Inland Revenue Estate Duty records* Public Record Office, Chancery Lane
*Inquisitions Post Mortem* Public Record Office, Chancery Lane
*Journal of the Bridge House Committee* Corporation of London Record Office
*Journal of the Common Council of the City of London* Corporation of London Record Office
*lay subsidy lists* Public Record Office, Chancery Lane
*Letters & Papers of the Reign of Henry VIII* Public Record Office, Chancery Lane
*Levant Company records* Public Record Office, Chancery Lane; Hertfordshire Record Office, County Hall, Hertford
*Lewis's Topographical Dictionary* public reference libraries
*lists of emigrants (published)* Society of Genealogists
*local newspapers* British Library Newspaper Library; local newspaper offices; some public libraries
*London Land Tax records* Guildhall Library MSS Department
*London livery company records* Guildhall Library
*London Trade Directory 1740* Guildhall Library; Society of Genealogists
*London Tradesman, The* British Library; Guildhall Library; Corporation of London Record Office
*London wardmote records* Guildhall Library
*manor court records* National Register of Archives, Quality House, Quality Court, Chancery Lane, London WC2; county record offices
*Man (and Maid) Servant Tax Assessments* county record offices
*maps* Public Record Office, Chancery Lane; British Library; county record offices; etc.
*maritime charts* National Maritime Museum, Greenwich, London SE10
*Members of Parliament, records of* in *History of Parliament*, major reference libraries
*Merchant Taylors printed history* Guildhall Library
*Methodist archives* Public Record Office, Chancery Lane; county record offices; Methodist Archives and Research Centre, 23-25 City Road, London EC1
*monumental inscriptions* county family history societies; Society of Genealogists
*muster book* Public Record Office, Chancery Lane
*muster certificates* Public Record Office, Chancery Lane
*National Register of Archives* Quality House, Quality Court, Chancery Lane, London WC2
*newspaper reports* British Library Newspaper Library
*non-conformist chapel registers* Public Record Office, Chancery Lane
*non-conformist, general* Dr Williams's Library, 14 Gordon Square, London WC1

*Operation Orders, World War I* Public Record Office, Kew
*Ordnance Survey maps, seventeenth-century* David & Charles (publishers), Newton Abbot, Devon
*Overseers of the Poor records* county record offices
*parish registers* county record offices
*parliamentary votes* see *poll books*
*parochial officers' records* county record offices
*Petitions to Parliament* House of Lords Record Office
*poll books* Guildhall Library; Society of Genealogists; county record offices
*poll tax lists* Public Record Office, Chancery Lane
*poor apprentice bindings* county record offices
*Presbyterian archives* Public Record Office, Chancery Lane; Presbyterian Historical Society, 14 Queen's Road, Barnet, Hertfordshire
*Presentments of the Guildable Manor, Southwark* Guildhall Library MSS Department
*private diaries* record offices; private collections
*probate inventories* Public Record Office, Chancery Lane; county record offices; Borthwick Institute of Historical Research,
*Protestation Oath returns* House of Lords Record Office
*Quaker archives* Friends' House, Euston Road, London NW1
*Quarter Sessions records* county record offices
*regimental histories* National Army Museum
*Register of Passports* Public Record Office, Kew
*Registers of Deaths & Burials Abroad* Public Record Office, Chancery Lane; county record offices
*Reports of Historical MSS Commission* offices of the Commission, Quality House, Quality Court, Chancery Lane, London WC2
*Reports on Former Monks & Nuns* Public Record Office, Chancery Lane
*Royal Indian Military College* India Office Library & Records
*school registers and logbooks, grammar* Society of Genealogists
-- *public* Society of Genealogists
-- *state* county record offices
*settlement papers* county record offices
*Sea Chirurgion, The* British Library
*slave registers* Public Record Office, Kew
*St Helena Factory Minutes* India Office Library & Records
*St John's, Hackney, Register of* Greater London Record Office
*St Olave's List of Inhabitants* Corporation of London Record Office
*St Olave's Precinct of Bridge Ward Within records* Corporation of London Record Office
*St Peter's, Cornhill, registers* Guildhall Library MSS Department
*St Peter's, Westcheap, registers* Guildhall Library MSS Department
*Star Chamber suits* Public Record Office, Chancery Lane
*State Papers* Public Record Office, Chancery Lane
*State Papers (Colonial)* Public Record Office, Chancery Lane
*State Papers (Domestic)* Public Record Office, Chancery Lane
*Statutes at Large* Greater London Record Office
*Statutes of the Realm* Public Record Office, Chancery Lane; major reference libraries
*tithe and enclosure awards* Public Record Office, Kew
*trade apprentice bindings* Public Record Office, Kew; Guildhall Library; Society of Genealogists; borough record offices
*Transactions of the Royal Historical Society* British Library
*transportation of petty thieves* Public Record Office, Kew; Guildhall Library; county record offices
*university registers* Society of Genealogists
*urban corporation records* borough or city record offices
*vestry minutes* county record offices
*Victoria County Histories* public reference libraries
*visitation records* county record offices
*ward and parish rate assessments* Guildhall Library MSS Department
*wills* Public Record Office, Chancery Lane; county record offices

# Index

Numbers in italics refer to illustrations.

# Picture credits

Tony Birks-Hay 36, 53, 98, 183; J. Campbell-Kease 20, 184; H.J.M. Stratton 183; Dorset County Record Office 22, 37, 44-5, 81, 84, 97, 125, 126; Mrs Janet Few 64; Miss A.D. Filliter and Dorset CRO 144-5; Terrick FitzHugh 76, 146, 179; David Flinn 27, 50, 102, 114; The Francis Frith Collection 89; Frome Society for Local Study 168; Guildhall Library, City of London 118; Mrs Noreen Hackett 183; Hereford & Worcester County Record Office 65; Crown copyright material in the Public Record Office is reproduced with the permission of the Controller of Her Majesty's Stationery Office (ref. HO 107/2146 folio 252 p.1) 86; The Incumbent and Parochial Church Council of Buckland Newton, and Dorset CRO 16; The Incumbent and Parochial Church Council of Hazlebury Bryan with Stoke Wake, and Dorset CRO 94; The Incumbent and Parochial Church Council of Wimborne Minster, and Dorset CRO 66; Mansell Collection 38, 47, 111; Museum of London 59; National Maritime Museum, London 115; The Gerald Pitman Sherborne Pictorial Record Collection 90, 136; L. Sayers 105; Westcountry Studies Library (Devon Library Services) 138; Mrs E. Wiltshire and Mr A. Knight 178; Courtesy Wymondham, Attleborough and Watton Methodist Circuits, in Norfolk Record Office 41.